WILLIAM SHAKESPEARE
IN 100
FACTS

ZOE BRAMLEY

Acknowledgements

I would like to thank Rob Woodford for giving me the idea for the chapter about Shakespeare's tree at Primrose Hill. As Black Cab Taxi Guide with www.blackcabheritagetours.co.uk his wealth of knowledge always comes in handy!

The chapters about Shakespeare's fools, the curse of Macbeth, and the Essex Rebellion were written by the fair hand of City of London Tour Guide Alan Aspinall. In true Shakespeare style, we collaborated on the chapter about Blackfriars.

The chapters on Edmund Shakespeare, the Bidford Sippers, and Wilton House are based on chapters included in my book *The Shakespeare Trail*.

It was Donald L. Holmes who first discovered that William Shakespeare is an anagram of 'I am a weakish speller.'

Contact me at @shakespearewalk

First published 2016

Amberley Publishing
The Hill, Stroud
Gloucestershire, GL5 4EP

www.amberley-books.com

British Library Cataloguing in Publication Data.
A catalogue record for this book is available from the British Library.

ISBN 978 1 4456 5624 3 (paperback)
ISBN 978 1 4456 5625 0 (ebook)

Typeset in 11pt on 13.5pt Sabon.
Typesetting and Origination by Amberley Publishing.
Printed in the UK.

CONTENTS

Introduction

William Shakespeare was unlucky enough to die on his birthday. He passed away on 23 April 1616 at home in Stratford-upon-Avon, a wealthy man with at least thirty-six plays to his name as well as sonnets and poems. Little could he have known that exactly 400 years later people across the globe would be planning a series of events to remember him. 2016 is set to bring a smorgasbord of museum exhibitions, TV adaptations of his plays and documentaries.

With such a busy Shakespeare schedule ahead, you may wish to have some bitesized Bard facts to hand. This is where this book steps in. In an exhilarating romp through 100 of the juiciest Shakespeare facts you will gain an overview of his life from beginning to end. We examine some of the conspiracy theories surrounding him and bust a few myths. Burning questions shall be answered: *Who wrote the plays?* (I'll answer this one now – Shakespeare did) *What did he do in the 'lost years'? Why did he steal a theatre?* We will also learn about how he nearly died of plague and the time he caused an ecological disaster in New York.

Shakespeare lived in exciting times. He witnessed the flowering of the English Renaissance and the union of the English and Scottish crowns. He helped revolutionise our language with timeless classics such as *Romeo and Juliet, Hamlet,* and *King Lear.* This book dives headlong into his world.

Shakespeare may have died 400 years ago but his genius burns as bright as ever.

1. WE KNOW NOTHING ABOUT WILLIAM SHAKESPEARE

It may seem cruel to begin a book called *William Shakespeare in 100 Facts* by saying we know nothing about him. You have been enticed with the promise of information about the man who wrote *Romeo and Juliet* and *Macbeth* only to be let down at the first chapter. 'What do you mean, we know nothing?' I hear you cry, 'We want facts, and plenty of them!'

Well, you shall have them.

A common piece of received 'wisdom' is that the facts of William Shakespeare's life are lost to history. We are informed that everything we think we know about him is supposition, the result of Chinese whispers handed down over the last 400 years. When was he born? Did he really write the plays? He is meant to be someone we will never know; a shadowy and intangible figure whose characters have more presence and vitality than their creator ever will.

Let's nip this in the bud with the first of our hundred facts: Shakespeare lived in an incredibly bureaucratic age. His birth, marriage and death are recorded. We have the mortgage deeds for a property he purchased in Blackfriars as well as the records of other property transactions in his native Stratford. Although he left no letters or diaries behind he is mentioned often enough by his contemporaries to begin building a picture of his life.

Over the next ninety-nine chapters you will begin to see exactly how much we really do know about the 'Sweet Swan of Avon'. Read on to find out!

2. William Shakespeare Was Born on St George's Day

William Shakespeare was born on 23 April 1564 in the Warwickshire town of Stratford-upon-Avon. We know this thanks to a scrawled line in the baptismal register of his local church, Holy Trinity, which records that Gulielmus filius Joahnnes Shakespeare (William, son of John Shakespeare) was baptised on 26 April. Babies were usually baptised around three days after their birth.

It is traditionally accepted that the place of his birth was a timber-framed house on Henley Street, which is located just off Stratford's bustling High Street. The house still stands today and is aptly known as the Birthplace. Here, baby Shakespeare was born into a middle-class family of farmers and glove makers. His father John operated a glove-making workshop in the family home and was an important figure in Stratford society, holding various important posts such as chamberlain, alderman, and even ale taster. His mother Mary was the daughter of a wealthy Warwickshire farmer. Her first two babies died in infancy but William's arrival in 1564 heralded a string of healthy children, five of which survived into adulthood.

As we all know, one of them would go on to become the most celebrated Englishman in history. In a career spanning the reigns of Elizabeth I and James I, Mary and John Shakespeare's first son would go on to write over thirty plays, helping to shape the English language as we know it.

With the knowledge of hindsight, the townsfolk of Stratford-upon-Avon might have celebrated this auspicious occasion, but if any ale was drunk on that happy day it would have been for quite a different reason. 23 April was also the feast of St George, England's patron saint. Although the Catholic tradition of keeping St George's Day as a public holiday had been outlawed in 1552 by the Protestant king Edward VI, folk memory still honoured the occasion. In towns across England the flag of St George – a red cross against a white background – could be seen fluttering in the breeze. It was traditional on St George's Day for the monarch to create new members of the Order of the Garter. This was a chivalric order which had adopted St George as their patron saint when it was established in 1348. Among those honoured by Elizabeth I on the day of Shakespeare's birth was the French king Charles IX.

Whether or not it was because they shared a special day, Shakespeare seemed to have an affinity for St George. One of the most rousing speeches in the 1599 play *Henry V* ends with the eponymous king leading his men into the Battle of Agincourt with the words 'Cry God for Harry, England and Saint George!' Shakespeare would have been aware that the historical soldiers wore the cross of St George on their tabards.

The modern St George's Day tends to be a muted affair in England, despite regular calls for it to be reinstated as a public holiday. Perhaps it is time to have a national William Shakespeare Day!

3. He Nearly Died of the Plague

William Shakespeare had been in the world for just three months when he was almost carried out of it again. On 11 July 1564 an apprentice named Oliver Gunne fell violently ill and died. He lived in the Degge family household on Sheep Street, a stone's throw from where Mary and John Shakespeare were nursing their newborn son. Presumably Oliver Gunne was cared for during his sickness by his master's wife, Joanna. Nine days later she died too. In the burial register of the parish church, Holy Trinity, a clerk wrote the fateful words: *hic incepit pestis*, or 'here begins the plague'.

The Stratford plague had claimed its first two victims in an outbreak which would go on to claim more than 200 lives. For a small town of 2,000 souls this was a devastating blow to the population. Almost every family would have lost someone, or been close to one of the victims. We don't know how the plague reached Stratford but the townsfolk were apparently infuriated to see the Town Clerk's servant walking around in public when he was showing symptoms. The plague lingered in Stratford for the remainder of the year, peaking that September before finally burning itself out by December when the cold frosts killed any remaining infection.

As the disease spread in that awful summer of 1564 a quick-thinking Mary Shakespeare is thought to have spirited her newborn baby William away to the safety of the countryside. Just think – if she had stayed in Stratford modern theatregoers could be attending the Royal Marlowe Theatre or Ben Jonson's Globe.

4. THE NEXT–DOOR NEIGHBOUR WAS A MAN CALLED GEORGE BADGER

In a town as small as Stratford it is to be expected that the Shakespeare family would have some good friends among the neighbours. One of these people was the interestingly named George Badger, a wool draper who lived right next door to the Shakespeares on Henley Street. The two residences were separated by a narrow strip of land, part of which Badger purchased from John Shakespeare in 1597 for £2. The two men had evidently been close friends for a number of years; they had something in common having both served as aldermen on the Stratford town council until they were kicked out for non-attendance. Rebellion seems to have run in Badger's blood; in 1578 he was fined for refusing to contribute funds towards a local militia.

Just as John Shakespeare's son would later leave Stratford to forge his dazzling career in London, George Badger's son Richard also packed up and headed for the bright lights of the capital, where he became apprentice to a stationer. The Stationer's Hall was located in the Blackfriars area of the city, just around the corner from a house which William Shakespeare would purchase in later life.

Back in Stratford, meanwhile, George Badger was getting himself into even more difficulty with the law. A committed Catholic, Badger was imprisoned for refusing to attend Protestant church services. All in all, William Shakespeare's boyhood neighbour seems to have been a bit of a wild card. Luckily his father John was much more conformist in nature – or was he?

5. His Father Was a Catholic Who Hid Illegal Tracts in the Rafters of the Family Home

One of the enduring controversies surrounding William Shakespeare is whether he adhered to the state religion, or whether he was a secret Catholic. Those who argue in favour of the latter point to the actions of his father at a time when so called 'papists' were viewed as Public Enemy Number One.

It all began in 1570, when the pope decided that Elizabeth I was a heretic. He excommunicated her and called on English Catholics to remove her from power if they could. Most Elizabethan Catholics were loyal to the crown and had no intention of becoming the pope's personal assassins, but nevertheless the authorities were jumpy. As far as the queen was concerned, those who gave their allegiance to the pope were potential terrorists who wanted her dead; Catholics were now viewed with suspicion and hostility. Elizabeth decided it was high time they proved their loyalty. The attendance of Anglican church services was made compulsory and anyone who refused was fined or imprisoned. She also began a purge on Catholic priests, making it illegal for them to enter the country. Anyone who was caught faced death by hanging, drawing and quartering. In 1581, despite the risk to his life, the Jesuit Edmund Campion travelled from Italy and sneaked into England to offer spiritual succour to the nation's beleaguered Catholics. He had in his possession copies of Cardinal Borromeo's 'Last Testament', a volume of essays professing the writer's Catholic faith. As Campion travelled through the Midlands, he distributed the pamphlets among members of the leading Catholic gentry with whom he lodged, gentlemen such as Sir William Catesby of Lapworth. Another recipient was John Shakespeare of Stratford, and he hid his copy well. John died in 1601, blissfully unaware that his secret would later be broadcast to the world.

The document remained hidden from prying eyes until 1757 when the occupant of the house at Henley Street – a descendant of Shakespeare's sister Joan – decided to get the roof fixed. Whilst rooting around in the attic the workmen discovered an ancient document concealed in the rafters. Each of its six pages bore the signature of John Shakespeare. It passed into the ownership of the gossipy Edmund Malone, an eighteenth-century Shakespeare biographer who published the document in his edition of the *Plays and Poems of William Shakespeare*. Malone later declared that it was a forgery, possibly out of a desire to think of England's greatest poet as coming from good Protestant stock. Unfortunately the 'Testament' is now lost so it cannot be examined, but it throws up some interesting questions about the Shakespeare family faith – if indeed they had one. It was John Shakespeare, after all, who oversaw the whitewashing of the medieval religious imagery in the Guild Chapel in 1563. If he was a Catholic, would he have done so in good conscience? Whether William retained any sympathies for Catholicism when he reached adulthood, he kept his ideas about religion close to his chest, which was probably the wisest thing to do.

6. His Mother Came from a Family Named After the Local Forest

Anyone who has read the 1599 comedy *As You Like It* will know that the action takes place in the Forest of Arden. It is an exotic place populated by lurking lions, snakes and young lovers who wander through the greenwood being witty and amusing. The Forest of Arden doesn't sound much like homely old Warwickshire – there are no palm trees where Shakespeare grew up – but as he described the antics of the heroes of the play, Rosalind, Celia and Orlando, his thoughts appear to have strayed to another forest; one much closer to home.

To the north of Stratford-upon-Avon was the real Forest of Arden, a huge wilderness of uncultivated countryside dotted with clumps of ancient oak trees. In the Middle Ages the forest had been covered by a thicket of trees. Travellers who ventured into its shadowy depths were at risk of attack from the robbers, outlaws and bandits who lurked there. With this in mind, it was traditional to stop and pray for safe passage at a stone cross located near the village of Coughton. By Shakespeare's day years of deforestation had gradually stripped the forest bare, opening it up to daylight and driving the shadows away. Arden still had a hold on the local imagination, however, and it is easy to see why Shakespeare had the forest in mind when he invented a hideout for the teenage runaways and outlaws of *As You Like It*.

His thoughts would also inevitably stray to his mother Mary. She was born Mary Arden, the youngest of eight sisters. Her childhood home was the village of Wilmcote, located deep within the Forest of

Arden. Her father Robert was a farmer who grew wealthy by renting pockets of his 150 acres of land to tenant farmers, one of whom was a certain Richard Shakespeare, grandfather to William. It was a crowded household – Mary and her sisters had to share a room with their stepmother's four children. The house was built in 1514, and visitors get a sense of how cramped the conditions would have been compared to the comforts we enjoy in the twenty-first century. All the girls slept upstairs on a wooden ledge reached by a ladder while the adults, Robert and his wife Agnes, slept in their own private chamber.

Despite their humble living arrangements the Ardens were rich in possessions. Robert Arden left behind an inventory of all his goods and chattels including eight oxen and a dovecote. They were also related to the Ardens of Park Hall, a very wealthy local family who would eventually find themselves in a bit of trouble with the law, as we shall see later.

In the meantime let us return to the Forest of Arden where Amiens will sing us out with some words about the innocent pleasures of forest life:

> Under the greenwood tree,
> Who loves to lie with me,
> And turn his merry note,
> Unto the sweet bird's throat,
> Come hither, come hither, come hither.
> Amiens, *As You Like It*, Act II, Scene V

We're on our way, Amiens.

7. His Least Favourite Subjects at School Were Latin and Greek

If we are to believe the playwright Ben Jonson, Shakespeare was a bit of a dunce when it came to the classical languages. In a brilliant example of the double-edged compliment, Jonson wrote a dedicatory poem to the 'Memory of My Beloved the Author, Mr William Shakespeare and What He Hath Left Us', in which he laments: 'Thou hadst small Latin and less Greek ...'

Jonson was liberal in his usage of Latin throughout his plays while Shakespeare stuck to the mother tongue, giving the impression that he was an egalitarian who never forgot his working-class audience. After all, if Shakespeare had small Latin and less Greek, then the groundlings standing in the pit of the Globe certainly did too. It is easy to imagine Jonson giving a patronising little smile as he wrote those lines, but was he correct?

As the son of an important figure in Stratford politics, Shakespeare would have received an education at the King's New School, the local grammar that was located on Chapel Street. The learning experience for an Elizabethan schoolboy was a gruelling ordeal. Lessons began at 6 a.m. and ran until 6 p.m. with just a two-hour break in the middle. Among the subjects crammed into the boys' heads via the tedious method of rote learning was – are you listening, Ben Jonson? – Latin. On the menu were Cicero, Ovid and Virgil. Discipline was harsh with the school masters meting out their beatings with frightening liberality. After enduring approximately ten years of this routine it is fair to say that Shakespeare knew Latin.

8. He Spent His Gap Year as a Private Tutor. Or an Actor. Or Was it a Pirate?

There are so many colourful theories about what Shakespeare got up to after leaving school it would take a lifetime to discuss them all. Let's have a look at some of the most popular ideas and see what we think of them.

He was an actor in a private household:
In 1581 a wealthy Lancashire gentleman called Alexander Hoghton left some intriguing instructions in his will. Bequeathing his collection of musical instruments and play clothes (theatrical costumes) to his half-brother Thomas Hesketh, he took care to secure the fate of the performers who might use these items. Hoghton's instructions were full of care and concern for the fate of two individuals in particular: 'If he will not keep players ... I most heartily require the said Sir Thomas to be friendly unto Fulk Gillam and William Shakeshafte now dwelling with me, and either to take them into his service or else help them to some good master.'

Could this mysterious William Shakeshafte have been the fifteen-year-old Shakespeare, fresh out of school? In later years the son of Kit Beeston, one of Shakespeare's fellow actors, claimed that Shakespeare had been a schoolmaster in a country house. Perhaps Thomas Hesketh had decided he didn't need players but would 'take them into his service' as tutors instead.

He travelled to Italy:
The huge numbers of foreign settings in Shakespeare's plays have given rise to a theory that he must have

spent time travelling abroad. Italy appears to have been a particular favourite of his; its various territories feature in no less that thirteen of the plays: *All's Well that Ends Well, Antony and Cleopatra, Coriolanus, Cymbeline, Julius Caesar, The Merchant of Venice, Much Ado About Nothing, Othello, Romeo and Juliet, The Taming of the Shrew, Titus Andronicus, The Two Gentlemen of Verona,* and *The Winter's Tale.* Phew!

It is tempting to think of him leaving school and then embarking on a grand tour of cities such as Venice, Verona and Milan, soaking up the Mediterranean atmosphere and finding inspiration which he would later use in his writing. The trouble with this idea is that his plays actually contain very little local colour. Let's face it – *Romeo and Juliet* could just as easily have been set in London. It was fashionable – not to mention wise in such a paranoid age – for Early Modern playwrights to use foreign settings; Ben Jonson and Christopher Marlowe also placed the action of their dramas in far-off lands.

This is not to say that Shakespeare didn't travel abroad but we should be wary of using his play settings as evidence that he did.

He was in London looking after horses:
The final theory is much less glamourous. In the eighteenth century, Samuel Johnson wrote that Shakespeare's first job in the theatre was to stand outside with the horses, keeping an eye on the beasts whilst their owners enjoyed the play. But enough horsing around – what was he doing with Sir Thomas Lucy's deer? Read on to find out.

9. HE ENJOYED PROWLING AROUND THE COUNTRYSIDE LOOKING FOR DEER (ALLEGEDLY)

According to legend, the young Shakespeare was something of a petty criminal. This slur on his reputation was started by a seventeenth-century clergyman, Richard Davies, who wrote that: 'Shakespeare was much given to all unluckiness in stealing venison and rabbits, particularly from Sir Lucy who oft had him whipped and sometimes imprisoned and at last made him fly his native country to his great advancement.'

The alleged victim of Shakespeare's illicit poaching activity was Sir Thomas Lucy of Charlecote House, located approximately five miles to the east of Stratford-upon-Avon. If we are to believe this story, we must imagine Shakespeare sneaking over there and hiding in Lucy's rolling parkland before trapping a deer and lugging it back home again. How many times he is supposed to have made the journey is unrecorded but legend says he was caught and effectively driven out of Warwickshire. It is a nice story and often shows up in the Shakespeare biographies but sadly it is almost certainly a myth. The deer park at Charlecote was only started in 1615 – one year before Shakespeare died.

That is not to say that Shakespeare had good relations with Lucy. There is an intriguing episode in *The Merry Wives of Windsor* in which Justice Shallow complains about Falstaff for poaching his deer. Shakespeare also makes a pun on Lucy's name when Shallow discusses the luces, or fish, which feature on his coat of arms. Shakespeare would have known that his nemesis Sir Thomas Lucy's coat of arms also featured luces. It was all very fishy.

10. HE ONCE GOT DRUNK BENEATH A TREE

One morning, after a night of heavy drinking, William Shakespeare is said to have woken up in the open air beneath a crab tree. His head must have been hurting, or maybe he was still tipsy, for that can be the only excuse for the bizarre lines of poetry that he is said to have uttered to his companions upon waking. Legend has it that the previous morning he had walked from Stratford to Bidford-on-Avon in search of the amiable local men who were renowned for their drinking competitions. On the way he had asked a shepherd where he could find the Bidford drinkers. The shepherd replied that they were absent – but would the Bidford sippers do instead? Shakespeare readily agreed that they would and went off to find them. After a night of carousing he collapsed underneath the crab tree to recover, only to be awoken the next morning by thirsty Bidford men imploring him to continue the session. Shakespeare declined but instead recited some strangely robotic lines about the local villages. He said he had drunk in:

Piping Pebworth, Dancing Marston,
Haunted Hillboro, Hungry Grafton,
Dodging Exhall, Papist Wixford,
Beggarly Broom and Drunken Bidford.

He clearly needed some painkillers.

'Drunken' Bidford lies on the Stratford to Evesham road with 'Beggarly' Broom just to the north. 'Hungry' Grafton may refer to Temple Grafton in the north east, and 'Dancing' Marston is probably Long Marston to the south west.

The story originated in 1762, when an anonymous letter was published in *The British Magazine* purporting to be from someone who had got the tale from a Stratford landlord acquainted with Shakespeare's descendants. It is a nice story and may be rooted in some truth, even if the details have been embellished along the way. The exact location of Shakespeare's crab tree has been forgotten as the tree was uprooted in 1824. Perhaps it stood somewhere along the banks of the River Avon. If the legend is true then Shakespeare may have followed the course of the river on the seven-mile-long walk from Stratford. Arriving into the village he would have seen the medieval packhorse bridge which dates from the early fifteenth century. Tradition has it that he met the Bidford sippers in the Old Falcon Inn, a huge gabled house on the corner of Church Street which dates from the mid-sixteenth century. Its stone façade hides a timber-framed section around the corner. The building has an interesting and varied history. As well as its time as an inn it has also functioned as a Victorian workhouse and an antiques centre.

Bidford is rightly proud of its Shakespeare heritage – on high days and holidays look out for the Shakespeare Morris Men who have performed in the local area since 1959, when they were formed by some alumni of Shakespeare's old school, King Edward VI School in Stratford.

On sunny days it is pleasant to sit by the riverbank and contemplate the possibility that 400 years ago, a young Shakespeare may have done the same.

11. He Married Anne Hathaway but His Heart Was Set on a Different Anne

In the autumn of 1582, when William Shakespeare reached the age of eighteen, he married a local farmer's daughter called Anne Hathaway. Anne lived in a timbered cottage at Newlands Farm in Shottery, a small village one mile outside Stratford-upon-Avon. With her father Richard having died the previous year and Anne still unmarried at the relatively mature age of twenty-six, she would have been keen to find a husband. Enter Shakespeare.

It is usually assumed that he had been a regular visitor to Newlands Farm that summer, perhaps helping with the harvest but almost certainly with his mind on more amorous matters. Anne fell pregnant in August and the couple married shortly afterwards. An intriguing hint of panic and 'last-minute rush' surrounds the Shakespeare marriage. On 27 November, two of Anne's farmer friends, Fulke Sandells and John Richardson, travelled to the consistory court at Worcester to apply for an emergency marriage licence on the couple's behalf. There was no time to lose – ecclesiastical law forbade wedding ceremonies to take place during Advent, a period which was fast approaching.

This is where it gets interesting. The name on the marriage licence is not Anne Hathaway of Shottery, but Anne Whateley of Temple Grafton. Was Shakespeare involved with another woman? Had he been planning to marry a different Anne all along? Romantic novelists might like to think so. There is, however, another, more plausible explanation for the two Annes.

The clerk who wrote 'Anne Whateley of Temple Grafton' had been working on another case involving someone else called Whately that day, so it is likely that his mind strayed and he made an honest mistake. The next day he signed the marriage bond and this time he got it right. Anne Hathaway of the parish of Stratford was now eligible to marry William Shakespeare. The location of the wedding ceremony is a mystery but some writers suggest that took place not in Stratford but in Temple Grafton, perhaps in an attempt to keep it low key and discourage any scandal which might arise out of Anne's pregnant state. It was not all that unusual for early-modern women to be pregnant upon their marriages but to have a child out of wedlock was certainly frowned upon. There was also a significant age difference between the pair. Shakespeare was eight years younger than Anne and, as a minor, had needed his parents' permission to marry. The young couple moved in with Shakespeare's parents at Henley Street where Anne gave birth to a daughter, Susannah, the following spring.

On the surface it would seem to be a functioning marriage but the Anne Whateley mystery has given fuel to those who imagine Shakespeare was a reluctant to wed her. In Anne Hathaway's defence, take a look at these lines from Sonnet 145:

'I hate' she altered with an end,
That followed it as gentle day,
Doth follow night, who like a fiend
From heaven to hell is flown away.
'I hate', from hate away she threw,
And saved my life, saying 'not you.'

If the sonnet refers to Anne Hathaway (or 'hate away') then it seems clear that she was the woman Shakespeare loved and she in turn quite liked him too.

12. The Chair in Which He Courted Anne Hathaway Can Still Be Seen

Speaking of Anne Hathaway, visitors to her cottage in Shottery may wish to pause in one of the upstairs chambers to examine a rather interesting curiosity. At first glance it looks like a simple oak armchair, but look more closely. Among the intricate carvings in the back panel of the chair, you will see the letters 'W A S', thought by some to stand for William and Anne Shakespeare. To the side of these mysterious letters is the carved image of a shield with a falcon and spear – the very image which adorns Shakespeare's coat of arms.

It cannot be proven but legend says that the Shakespeare buttocks once rested upon this very item.

It was the eighteenth-century author Samuel Ireland who first discovered the chair during a visit to the cottage in 1792. The resident John Hart, a descendent of Shakespeare's sister Joan, told him it had 'always in his remembrance been called Shakespeare's courting chair'. Believing this to be the very chair upon which Shakespeare reclined whilst romancing his future wife, Ireland purchased it and brought it home to London where he proudly showed it off to intrigued visitors. His son William Henry was more sceptical and decided to poke fun at those who flocked to see it. In 1795 the notorious prankster forged a 'lost' Shakespeare play which he called *Vortigern and Rowena* and made guests sit upon the revered chair whilst he read it aloud, all the time trying to restrain his laughter.

The chair later went missing but the Shakespeare Birthplace Trust stumbled upon it at auction in 2002.

13. If it Hadn't Been for a Fatal Brawl in 1587 We May Never Have Heard of William Shakespeare

One of the great mysteries about Shakespeare's life is how he escaped from sleepy Stratford to become a star of the London stage. In over 300 years of Shakespeare scholarship, the best theory anyone has come up with is one which involves two angry men and a sharp sword.

It was the summer of 1587. London's premier troupe of actors had embarked on a tour, bringing their repertoire of hit plays to the provinces. It would have been a dazzling spectacle; after all, the Queen's Men were Elizabeth I's very own theatre company. The players wore rich scarlet and boasted some of the finest acting talent in the capital, with famous names such as the comedian Richard Tarleton and the actor John Heminges. Their plays included titles such as *Friar Bacon and Friar Bungay* by Robert Greene and the anonymous *Famous Victories of Henry V*, a play which would later inspire Shakespeare. This was a company coated in stardust. To understand how excited an ordinary small-town Elizabethan might have been to see the Queen's Men in town, imagine Elton John or Madonna playing a concert in Bognor Regis.

We know they passed through Stratford-upon-Avon, but before that they stopped in the little town of Thame in Oxfordshire. This is where it all went wrong. The actor who played Henry V in the *Famous Victories* was a short-tempered man called William Knell. We know he was quick to anger because on the night of 13 June, possibly after a bout of heavy drinking, he attacked his fellow actor John Towne with a sword.

The scene was White Hound Close, located behind the inn-yard theatre in which the company had been performing. Knell was seen brandishing his sword at Towne who wisely fled. Knell gave chase. We don't know why they were arguing but we do know that one of them would soon be dead. According to the coroner's report, 'William Knell, continuing his attack as before, so maliciously and furiously, Towne ... to save his life drew his sword (price five shillings) and held it in his right hand and thrust it into the neck of William Knell and made a mortal wound three inches deep and one inch wide.'

The Queen's Men had previous form when it came to acts of violence. In 1583, John Singer and John Bentley murdered an audience member in Norwich for not paying their entry fee.

A few days after Towne and Knell's fatal brawl, the undoubtedly demoralised Queen's Men limped into Stratford–upon-Avon. The exact date of their arrival is unrecorded but they may have performed at the Guildhall or in one of the many inn-yard theatres. Two men down, with Knell dead and Towne in gaol, they had a long tour ahead of them. Was this the moment a young William Shakespeare stepped out of rural obscurity to take his place on the world stage? It is tempting to think so.

14. Shakespeare Was No 'University Wit'

Elizabethan London was teeming with creative talent and Shakespeare would have quickly felt at home. Among those making a living from their quill pens were dramatists such as Christopher Marlowe, Robert Greene, John Lyly, George Peele, and Thomas Lodge. Not only were they talented, they were highly educated. Marlowe, Greene and Nashe had all gone to Cambridge University, while Peele, Lyly and Lodge were Oxford graduates. In the nineteenth century the writer George Saintesbury described the sextet collectively as the 'University Wits'. Saintesbury viewed these playwrights as being quite distinct from those such as Henry Chettle and Anthony Munday, who had entered the profession from less academic routes. Lacking the prestige of a degree these were men who 'boast(ed) Shakespeare as their chief'.

With little more than a stint at Stratford Grammar behind him, Shakespeare was about to embark on a steep learning curve.

If we accept that he arrived in London in 1587 as a new member of the Queen's Men the young Warwickshire lad might have seen Marlowe's groundbreaking play *Tamburlaine the Great*, which was performed that year by the Admiral's Men. Around this time Thomas Kyd wrote *The Spanish Tragedy*, a hugely popular play which would be revived again and again over the succeeding decades. The standard of the University Wits' writing was formidable but, despite Shakespeare's lack of a higher education, he was soon to surpass them all. Shortly after his arrival in the capital he took his first steps in playwriting with *Henry VI*. At this point, one of the University Wits started to take a strong dislike to him ...

15. HE WAS AN 'UPSTART CROW' AND A 'JACK OF ALL TRADES'

Robert Greene MA, alumnus of Cambridge, was famous for many things. For a start, he was the author of the catchily titled *Friar Bacon and Friar Bungay*, a raucous comedy about magic and seduction. It featured regularly in the repertoires of the playing companies throughout the 1590s, attesting to its popularity. Greene was also something of a poet, a romantic prose writer, and pamphleteer (the Elizabethan equivalent of a Fleet Street hack). Like some of his modern day descendants in the print trade, Greene was fond of a drink. Constantly in debt, he spent his wife's dowry and then promptly deserted her in order to move in with a prostitute, the sister of a small-time crook nicknamed 'Cutting Ball'. The happy couple had an illegitimate son whom they named Fortunatus.

It was a tough, sordid life but something else was troubling Robert Greene. In the late summer of 1592, he picked up his quill and began to put this latest grievance into words. Although his health was fading he managed to summon the energy to write a delicious rant which caused uproar upon its publication. He did not live to see the fallout, dying of a 'surfeit of pickled herrings and rhenish wine' on 3 September, but three weeks after his death Greene's final pamphlet dropped like a bomb on London. It was titled *Groatsworth of Wit, Bought with a Million of Repentance* and was a piece so scathing and bitter it throws a light on the literary rivalries of the day. It also gives us some important clues about Shakespeare and his whereabouts.

One of the passages in the *Groatsworth* is a densely

worded complaint about actors: 'Those puppets, I mean, that spake from our mouths, those anticks garnished in our colours ... trust them not.' Greene's scorn drips like venom. He goes on to rail against one actor in particular who has had the nerve to try his hand at writing: 'There is an upstart crow, beautified with our feathers, that with his tyger's heart wrapped in a player's hide, supposed he is as well able to bombast out a blanke verse as the best of you: and being an absolute Johannes fac totum, is in his own conceit the only Shake-scene in a country.'

The mystery victim sounds an awful lot like the author of *Henry VI: Part III;* Greene's reference to a 'tyger's hart wrapped in a player's hide' comes directly from a scene in which York tells Margaret she has a 'tiger's heart wrapped in a woman's hide.' Anyone who had seen the play would know that Shakespeare was the target of this diatribe, but if it was not obvious enough he practically names him by referring to 'Shake-scene'.

It appears that Shakespeare (or someone) took great offence to Greene's pamphlet as the printer, Henry Chettle, felt obliged to issue an apology for his part in its production. Robert Greene may have died penniless and bitter but he ensured his name would be entangled with Shakespeare's for eternity.

16. William Shakespeare is an Anagram of 'I Am a Weakish Speller'

Shakespeare was indeed a weakish speller and I shall attempt to prove it here.

Exhibit A: When Shakespeare signed a court document in 1612 he abbreviated his signature to Shakp. Either he was trying to save time or he couldn't spell his name. Consider the following variants of his name when he was purchasing property in Blackfriars and signing his will: Shaksper, Shakespe, Shakspere and Shakspeare. He nearly got there with that last one! The only time his name appears as 'Shakespeare' is in his printed signature that appears on the front page of the poem *Venus and Adonis*.

Exhibit B: The spelling in his plays. I give you the first few lines of *Romeo and Juliet* as an example. This is from an edition printed in 1599:

> Two households, both alike in dignitie,
> (In faire Verona where we lay our Scene),
> From auncient grudge, break to new mutinie,
> Where civill bloud makes civill hands uncleane.

Bottom of the class, Shaksper!

To be fair to Shakespeare (or Shakpe), he was not the only Elizabethan without a dictionary. Dedicating lines to Shakespeare in the First Folio, his friend Ben Jonson spelled Britain as Britaine and out-do as out-doo.

The English language was not yet standardised so writers spelled words the way they were pronounced. This gives a fascinating insight into Early Modern pronunciation. The confusion over spelling seems to have amused Shakespeare. In *Love's Labour's*

Lost, Holofernes insists on the pronunciation of the redundant 'B' in 'debt' and 'doubt'.

Verdict: Shakespeare may have been a 'weakish speller' but he wrote Macbeth so we forgive him.

17. The Works of Shakespeare Were Written by Christopher Marlowe, Francis Bacon and Elizabeth I (Not!)

As we saw earlier, Robert Greene was not exactly Shakespeare's biggest fan. He did, however, believe that William Shakespeare was the author of his own plays, affording him a bigger favour than many of his modern day admirers. In recent years a huge industry has grown up around the strange belief that the works of Shakespeare were written by anyone except, well, Shakespeare. Let's examine some of the alternative candidates for the authorship and hopefully put them to rest.

Christopher Marlowe: The precociously talented Marlowe was Shakespeare's exact contemporary. Both men were born in 1564 and both came from similar backgrounds – Shakespeare was a glover's son and Marlowe was a cobbler's son. The main difference is that Marlowe had the advantage of a university education and it is for this reason that some people prefer to think that the Shakespeare canon was written by Marlowe instead. The fact that Marlowe died in Deptford in 1593 before Shakespeare had even written very much does not deter them. These conspiracy theorists assert that Marlowe faked his own death and escaped to the continent in order to write the plays under the name 'Shakespeare'. When asked why he would go to so much trouble – why not stay in London and write the plays in his own name? – they invent fantastical scenarios. As one of Thomas Walsingham's spies, he 'knew too much'. He was in danger of his life. To which, the level-headed reader replies: 'Exactly! That is why he was murdered in Deptford in 1593!'

Edward de Vere, the Earl of Oxford: In 1920 the writer J. Thomas Looney threw a new candidate into the ring with his book *Shakespeare Identified in Edward de Vere, 17th Earl of Oxford*. He argued that someone raised in a country town like Stratford-upon-Avon would have neither the intellect nor education to write such stunning pieces of work. Looney saw a bias towards the aristocratic characters in the plays and on this basis decided that only a nobleman could have written them. We might counter by asking whether a Tudor aristocrat could write so vividly about ordinary folk. Shakespeare, the country boy, certainly could. It is true that Edward de Vere was an accomplished poet in his own right; works such *Sitting Alone Upon My Thought* and *What Cunning Can Express* were celebrated among his contemporaries. Unfortunately, the earl died in 1604, making it impossible for him to have written *Macbeth, King Lear, The Tempest* or *Othello*.

Anne Whateley: Unfortunately this is not a joke. In 1939 the author William Ross wrote *The Story of Anne Whateley and William Shaxper* in which he argued that the mysterious Anne Whateley – a woman who probably did not even exist – was the author of Shakespeare's sonnets and poems. Through a close reading of the texts Ross deduced that Whateley was a nun who met Shakespeare when he visited her at her convent. The pair planned to marry but were thwarted when Anne Hathaway announced that she was pregnant. I'm saying nothing.

18. The Man Who Paid for *Venus and Adonis* and *The Rape Of Lucrece* Had a Cat Named Trixie

Yes, it's true. Henry Wriothesley, 3rd Earl of Southampton, had a cat named Trixie but that's just one of the many interesting things about him. It was Southampton who gave the young playwright William Shakespeare a leg up at the start of his career. When Shakespeare completed the poem *Venus and Adonis* in around 1593 he aimed high and dedicated it to the earl even though he was unsure how it would be received: 'I know not how I shall offend in dedicating my unpolished lines to your lordship, nor how the world will censure me for choosing so strong a prop.' Whether this display of modesty was real or feigned, Southampton liked the poem enough to accept another one, *The Rape of Lucrece*, which Shakespeare prefaced with even more gushing compliments: 'The love I dedicate to your lordship is without end.'

This early patronage makes the earl an important figure in the story of Shakespeare – but let's get back to Trixie. Southampton loved his cat so much he posed with it in a 1603 portrait. They make a very fine pair. Southampton stands in the Tower of London having been arrested for trying to overthrow the queen, his arm in a sling. His long auburn hair billows out around his shoulders, framing the pale, serious features of a man who has just had a close escape from the headsman's axe. Trixie the black and white pussycat perches on the window sill behind her dashing, noble master, proving that even macho Elizabethans took comfort and joy from their pets.

19. He Had an Affair with a Brothel Keeper and a 'Lovely Boy'

Shakespeare's life in London was not 'all work and no play'. In between what must have been some exhausting bouts of writing, according to some scholars he may have managed to make time for some extramarital fun. Our clues to his allegedly lurid love life come from the sonnets in which he writes passionately about both a 'Dark Lady' and a 'Fair Youth'.

The Fair Youth: The theme of Sonnets 1–126 deals with the importance of marriage and procreation. This is Shakespeare's attempt at persuading a reluctant young man to tie the knot. The subject's identity is unknown but one of the commonly favoured candidates is William Herbert, 3rd Earl of Pembroke who was under pressure to marry the daughter of Shakespeare's patron Henry Carey, the Lord Chamberlain. Whoever this 'fair youth' was, the sequence of sonnets dedicated to him sometimes veers into homoerotic territory. Take these lines from Sonnet 20:

> A woman's face with nature's own hand painted,
> Hast thou, the master mistress of my passion.

After comparing his looks and character favourably with women, he ends by lamenting the youth's male anatomy:

> But since she prick'd thee out for women's pleasure,
> Mine be thy love and thy love's use their treasure.

Sonnet 126 is even more direct, calling him 'my lovely boy'. The clues to Shakespeare's sexuality do not end with the sonnets. In *The Merchant of Venice* the character Antonio is widely believed to be in love with Bassanio, and the plot of *Twelfth Night* spins on cross-dressing seduction. Is this a sign that Shakespeare had gay affairs? Possibly, but the true answer is that we'll never know.

The Dark Lady: The star of Sonnets 127–152 is a mysterious woman with whom Shakespeare appears to be madly in love. Some of his best-loved lines are written in her honour, such as these from Sonnet 130:

> My mistress' eyes are nothing like the sun,
> Coral is far more red than her lips red;
> If snow be white, why then her breasts are dun;
> If hair be wires, black wires grow upon her head.

On the face of it, Shakespeare appears to be describing a black woman and some writers have identified her as 'Black Luce' or 'Lucy Negro' who ran a brothel on St John's Street in Clerkenwell. There seems to some confusion, however, as Lucy has also been identified as Lucy Morgan, a Welshwoman who was a lady in waiting at the court of Elizabeth I before she changed career and opened her brothel. Known as an 'arrant whore and a bawde', she and her girls appeared on stage at Gray's Inn in 1594 to the delight of the law students. The entertainment was the Prince of Purpoole, and with tongues firmly in cheek Lucy was presented as the Abbess of Clerkenwell, a mocking nod to the dissolved nunnery on whose grounds her brothel was located.

Lucy Morgan is not the only candidate for Shakespeare's 'Dark Lady' but she is certainly one of the most intriguing.

20. Shakespeare Wanted to Keep His Sonnets Private

With such personal subject matter it is little wonder that Shakespeare wanted to keep the sonnets private. Writing in 1598, the Elizabethan author Francis Meres referred to them as 'sugared sonnets among his private friends', giving the impression that their circulation was confined to a small circle of Shakespeare's intimate acquaintances.

If we take the sonnets as autobiographical, they can be seen as a window into Shakespeare's heart; something to be closely guarded from public view.

Imagine his unease then, when an enterprising publisher got hold of them. William Jaggard was an up-and-coming printer and publisher who worked from his shop at the Barbican. It was a handy location, for not far away was St Paul's Churchyard where the Elizabethan book trade had its headquarters. Wooden stalls lined the outside of the cathedral, selling everything from volumes of poetry, religious tracts and, of course, play texts. It was here in 1599 that Jaggard launched *The Passionate Pilgrim*, a collection of twenty poems which included two of Shakespeare's sonnets plus three poems which had appeared in his play *Love's Labour's Lost*. The other poems are mostly by anonymous authors – we don't know who they are – but Jaggard attributed them all to Mr W. Shakespeare. He clearly had pound signs in his eyes; Shakespeare was hot stuff.

Far from being flattered at being used as a cash cow for the print trade, we might imagine that Shakespeare was furious.

In 1609 he took control of his work by publishing

the sonnets himself in a collection called, simply, *Shakespeare's Sonnets*. The book was dedicated to a Mr W. H., usually assumed to be either William Herbert (purported to be the Fair Youth of the sonnets) or his patron Henry Wriothesley, the 3rd Earl of Southampton (albeit with his initials inexplicably reversed).

But Jaggard was not yet finished with Shakespeare. In 1612 he reprinted *The Passionate Pilgrim* incurring the poet's wrath once more. Although we have no record of Shakespeare's own reaction to the theft of his work, a compelling clue comes from his fellow playwright Thomas Heywood. In this later edition of *The Passionate Pilgrim*, Jaggard included some poems that he knew were by Heywood but he omitted Heywood's name, making the title page of the collection appear as if Shakespeare was the sole author of the works within. Shakespeare had the Elizabethan version of a star billing; he was an 'A Lister' with his name in lights. Touchingly, Heywood worried that readers would think that he and Shakespeare had plagiarised each other. He described Shakespeare's exasperation: 'So the author I know much offended with Jaggard (that altogether unknown to him) presumed to make so bold with his name.' In response, Jaggard removed Shakespeare's name from the unsold copies. This debacle does not seem to have harmed his printing career; after Shakespeare died Jaggard was commissioned to print the First Folio of his plays.

Jaggard may have 'made bold' with Shakespeare's name but posterity thanks him. After all, what's a 'sugared sonnet' between friends?

21. SHAKESPEARE WAS A TAX EVADER

Shakespeare was annoyed with William Jaggard, but he was not such an angel himself.

In twenty-first-century Britain tax evaders are rather frowned upon. They are labelled as tight-fisted, selfish dodgers of civic duty who enjoy public services but refuse to pay for them. Who would want to be a tax dodger? Whether by oversight or design, Shakespeare did. That's right, for a brief period in the 1590s, our best-loved poet, that 'Sweet Swan of Avon', became the type of person that HMRC might be obliged to chase for unpaid revenue.

Before we rush to damn him as a grasping scrooge, however, let's consider that it may not have been his fault. Shakespeare's first known address in London was somewhere in the parish of Bishopsgate to the north-east of the City. We know this because in 1598 his name appeared in the Bishopsgate Subsidy Rolls, a list signifying how much each resident was worth and therefore how much tax they were required to cough up. Shakespeare was assessed on £5 worth of personal wealth out of which he was charged thirteen shillings and four pence. This was a cumulative sum which had been building up since 1596. Unfortunately for the tax collectors, they were unable to find him at his address. It was around this time that his theatre company, the Chamberlain's Men, were moving their operations to Bankside on the south bank of the River Thames. Unbeknownst to the authorities, Shakespeare had left the parish, shifting himself to Bankside where the Globe Playhouse was in construction. In the upheaval of the move, his tax liabilities appear to have slipped his mind.

So how might his contributions have been spent? The subsidy for which he was being chased was a tax which was introduced by parliament to bolster the finances of the crown. To put it crudely, Shakespeare and his fellow citizens were being asked to help fund Elizabeth I's dress collection. One of the other tax burdens on Elizabethans came from the 1563 Act for the Relief of the Poor, a type of safety net designed to ensure that nobody starved to death. It decreed that all citizens who had the means should pay something towards the upkeep of the local homeless and destitute. Under the provisions of the act, beggars were licensed and were required to wear a badge to identify themselves and shame the wealthy into increasing their contributions. Anyone who failed to pay their share could be fined.

Although Shakespeare had still not reached the midway point of his career in 1598, it seems he was already richer than two of his colleagues in the Chamberlain's Men. The Subsidy Rolls of 1598 tell us that Richard and Cuthbert Burbage, sons of theatre impresario James Burbage, were only worth £3 and £4 respectively in comparison to Shakespeare's £5.

If you worry that Shakespeare was rubbing his hands in glee whilst hoarding cash, fear not. The tax collectors eventually caught up with him on Bankside and extracted the shillings he owed.

22. *Romeo and Juliet* Was the First Play about Romantic Love

Although the play *Romeo and Juliet* is classed as a tragedy (spoiler alert: they both die), the narrative is infused with the heady scent of romance and it is fairly natural to think of the play as a crossover between the two genres. In Act I, Scene V, Shakespeare became a pioneer when he introduced the first ever romantic kiss to feature on stage. In fact, he devoted much of the scene to a discussion on kissing. Here is a taster:

> Romeo: (Taking Juliet's hand) If I profane with my
> Unworthiest hand
> This holy shrine, the gentle sin is this:
> My lips, two blushing pilgrims, ready stand
> To smooth that rough touch with a tender kiss.

After a bit of snogging Juliet compliments Romeo on his technique:

> Juliet: You kiss by th' book.

No playwright of Shakespeare's generation had ever presented kissing on stage before. That is not to say that romance was a new genre – it wasn't. The poet Geoffrey Chaucer had written the romantic tale of *Troilus and Criseyde* almost 200 years before Shakespeare dreamt of putting a pair of star-cross'd lovers on stage. In fact the story of *Romeo and Juliet* was not even his. It derived from an old Italian tale about Romeo, Giuletta and the feuding Montecchi and Capuletti families. Shakespeare's source would have been *The Tragicall Historye of Romeus and Juliet*, a poem written in 1562 by Arthur Brooke. Shakespeare took the skeleton of Brooke's poem and dressed it up with vivid characters such as Mercutio. With his artist's flair he managed to turn what had been a dull, monotonous narrative into a thrilling drama fit for the stage.

If Shakespeare adapted *Romeo and Juliet* to his own tastes then generations of theatre producers and film makers have done likewise, bringing to the fore a range of fascinating versions. Probably the most famous film version of the play was *Romeo + Juliet* (1996) by the Australian director Baz Luhrmann. Starring Leonardo di Caprio as Romeo and Claire Danes as Juliet, the action takes place in a fictional American city called Verona Beach. The contemporary soundtrack underscores the timelessness of the play's themes of passionate love and hate.

In 2010 the Royal Shakespeare Company launched an experimental version of the play using the relatively new medium of Twitter. *Such Tweet Sorrow* was performed via a series of 4,000 tweets from a small cast of actors. They improvised as they went along using their own words, for example Juliet (@julietcap16) who tweeted gems such as 'OMG ... did anyone else just see the gorgeous boy in the funny mask who just walked past me...? Am I dreaming?' and 'OMG my Dad is so ANNOYING! I need to see Romeo! I'm not going to Australia ...' It was an interesting experiment, if not universally loved by the critics. As Michael Billington of the Guardian pointed out, the real WS is more about poetry than plot.

OMG, he's right about that!

23. The First Person to Play Juliet Was a Boy

We have such an abundance of amazing Shakespearean actresses – Judi Dench, Frances Barber et al – it is difficult to imagine a time when characters such Juliet and Cleopatra were played by boys.

In Shakespeare's day it was not the done thing for women to appear on the public stage. There was no explicit law banning them from appearing, but in reality it was unthinkable for a woman to strut her stuff on a platform in front of thousands of people. In a chauvinistic age the fairer sex was expected to be meek and modest. It was bad enough for male actors who were looked down upon as disreputable people. Elizabethan and Jacobean London was a magnet for creative and eccentric types, however, so there was an interesting exception to this rule. In 1611, a pickpocket and brothel keeper named Mary Frith (or Moll Cutpurse) appeared on stage at the Fortune Theatre in Finsbury. She was a cross-dresser and stood up on stage in male garb complete with doublet, breeches and boots, where she exchanged ribaldries with the delighted crowd. Nobody expected meekness from Moll Cutpurse. A more genteel form of female acting could be seen at court where aristocratic ladies performed in an elaborate entertainment called the Masque. These were characterised by their rich scenery and music. It was not a form of entertainment which ever attracted Shakespeare.

On the public stage the theatre companies used boy actors to represent women. Their unbroken voices and slight frames made them the perfect substitute. Shakespeare made reference to them in Act II, Scene II of *Hamlet* when the eponymous hero asks Rosencrantz about the practice of using boy players: 'What, are they children? Who maintains 'em? How are they escorted? Will they pursue the quality no longer than they can sing?' Hamlet is concerned about whether the boys will still be able to earn a living. He needn't have worried. When their voices broke, the talented ones could look forward to a long and prosperous career. Kit Beeston started his career as a child actor, apprenticed to Augustine Phillips, Shakespeare's fellow shareholder in the Chamberlain's Men. Beeston thrived and in later years became a theatre manager in his own right.

Not all boys had such a gentle start as Beeston; it was not unknown for playhouse employees to snatch them from the street and press them into service. Nathan Field was taken and put to work with the Children of the Chapel who performed at Blackfriars. Another boy who found himself drafted into service was Solomon Pavy who was abducted whilst walking home from school. His father complained bitterly in the Star Chamber and won his son back. Entertainment was a serious business.

It would be nice to know who that first Juliet was, or that first Lady Macbeth, Titania or Rosalind. Some of them will have lived to see the first actresses take to the stage in the mid-seventeenth century and the beginning of a new era.

24. Shakespeare Helped to Steal a Theatre

It wasn't just any old theatre either. This was The Theatre, the first purpose built playhouse in London and the venue in which young Shakespeare cut his teeth as a playwright. It was located in Shoreditch outside the City of London, the first of three playhouses in those semi-rural northern suburbs. You may think it was a strange idea to build a theatre in the middle of nowhere; even today it would be unusual. After all, the customers are in the City, right? Well, that's true, but Elizabethan theatre makers were not very popular with the City authorities. They saw the playhouses as dens of iniquity where people gathered in great numbers to indulge in vice and sin. In 1575 the Puritans banned them from the City so they simply moved outside to the 'liberties' of London, areas outside the control of interfering authority. In this way, several new entertainment districts began to evolve.

Built by James Burbage in 1576, The Theatre was a polygonal structure with three-tiered galleries and an open yard from where 'groundlings' – those who could not afford a seat – gazed up at the action on stage. The rich and the aristocratic had the option of paying for their own private boxes. A Puritan preacher called The Theatre 'a gorgeous playing place erected in the fields'. Believe it or not, he was trying to disparage it. This gorgeous playing place was built in the grounds of the old Holywell priory, a religious house which had been dissolved during the reign of Henry VIII. The land belonged to a man called Giles Allen, who gave Burbage a twenty-year lease with the option to renew for a further five years at the end. When 1596 came around, and the twenty-year lease was up, Allen refused to renew it so Burbage began law proceedings. There was a real risk that Shakespeare's company, the Chamberlain's Men, would become homeless. Luckily they were able to move into a temporary home, the nearby Curtain. Burbage died the following year – perhaps with the stress of it all. At this point his sons Richard and Cuthbert made an important decision. The timbers of The Theatre belonged to them, not Giles Allen. It was true they could no longer use his land, but surely there was nothing to stop them from taking the building.

On a cold night in December 1598, a group of players, probably including Shakespeare, gathered outside The Theatre. They were armed with swords and rapiers and had with them a team of carpenters who quickly dismantled the playhouse, which was then stored in a warehouse on the banks of the River Thames. The following spring, they shipped the materials over the river onto Bankside and rebuilt it. The Theatre was reborn as the Globe and would see the first performances of some of Shakespeare's finest writing.

As for Giles Allen, he tried to sue but his efforts were in vain. This is how Shakespeare stole a theatre.

25. Julius Caesar Opened the Globe Playhouse

Unfortunately it was not the Roman Emperor himself who opened the Globe but someone dressed very like him. As with all things Shakespeare we can never be 100 per cent certain of some of the facts, but it appears as if the first play to be performed at the Chamberlain's Men's new playhouse was the tragedy *Julius Caesar*. The clue comes thanks to a Swiss traveller called Thomas Platter who visited London in 1599. Luckily, he happened to be an avid diarist and made detailed notes about his trip. One entry in particular has been invaluable to scholars of theatre history. He wrote:

> On September 21st, after lunch about two o'clock, I and my party crossed the water, and there in the house with the thatched roof witnessed an excellent performance of the tragedy of the first Roman Emperor Julius Caesar with a cast of some fifteen people; when the play was over, they danced very gracefully together as is their wont, two dressed as men and two as women.

Thomas Platter also described such London delights as cockfighting, 'the feathers are full of blood', and bearbaiting contests in which mastiffs were 'struck and mauled by the bear'. Violent death was a fact of life in Elizabethan England; nobody worried about animal rights.

Back at the Globe, it must have been a relief for the Chamberlain's Men when their new playhouse opened its doors in 1599. At last they had a permanent home. It was built on Bankside near an existing playhouse, the Rose, where the Admiral's Men played. Like its forebear The Theatre, the Globe was polygonal in shape and came complete with tiered galleries that circled around an open-air yard topped with a thatched roof. It had capacity for 3,000 people, each of whom paid their entrance fee into a box as they entered. Those audience members who could afford a seat in the galleries were protected from the elements by the overhanging thatch. It was easy to tell what type of play was on offer by looking for the colour-coded flags outside: black for tragedy, red for history and white for comedy. Above the door was the inscription *totus mundus agit histrionem*, meaning 'all the world's a stage', echoing the line in Jacques' speech in the play *As You Like It* which was also written that year.

The Globe has become the playhouse most closely linked with Shakespeare and for good reason. Over the next fifteen or so years in which he was actively writing, the playhouse hosted performances of plays such as *Henry V, Romeo and Juliet, Measure for Measure,* and *Macbeth*. If indeed the first play to be performed there was *Julius Caesar* then the first words spoken in that cathedral of drama would have been the not very hospitable lines from Act I, Scene I:

Hence! Home you idle creatures, get you home!'

It is to be assumed that, having paid their pennies, the good people of London stayed right where they were.

26. Henry VIII Closed the Globe Playhouse

The original Globe playhouse dominated the Bankside theatre scene for fourteen glittering years but its end came quickly. It was 26 June 1613, a summer's afternoon. The playhouse was filled to capacity with a hungry crowd waiting for the drama to begin. Without realising it, they were also waiting for the drama to end.

Elizabeth I had died ten years before and James I was now on the throne. James had taken over the patronage of Shakespeare's company, effectively giving them elevated status as servants to His Majesty. It was a definite promotion and they were the hottest ticket in town. On that fateful day they were presenting a new play, *Henry VIII*. Since the tyrannical king of the six wives was Elizabeth I's father, Shakespeare would never have been allowed to dramatise his reign when the queen was alive. Now was his opportunity to present the tangled story of Anne Boleyn, Katherine of Aragon and Cardinal Wolsey. It was fairly recent history and shocking enough to make for a good play.

What happened on that summer's day at the Globe could easily have been avoided. After all, common sense says it's not a good idea to fire a cannonball in an enclosed wooden space. But this was drama! Bring on the cannons! In one of the scenes, Henry VIII enters Cardinal Wolsey's house. On that fateful day (never since) the King's Men duly fired a cannon in his honour. A stray spark landed in the thatched roof and began slowly burning its way around the circumference. Nobody noticed; they were too enthralled in the drama. The roof began to smoulder. Eyewitness Henry

Wooten wrote later that the audience thought it 'but an idle smoak' and turned their attention back to the play. Big mistake. In less than an hour the wooden playhouse had burnt to the ground. Nobody died but one man's breeches caught fire. A ballad written shortly afterwards describes a scene of mayhem as people fled:

Out run the knights: out run the lords
And then there was great ado
Some lost their hats and some lost their swords
Then out ran Burbage too

It goes on to describe the actor John Heminges stuttering in distress as he watches his life's work burn to the ground. It was a disaster, but the King's Men were a resilient bunch and quickly began work on a new building which was completed the following year. This time they erred on the side of caution and gave it a tiled roof to try and prevent any more accidents. After the Great Fire of London of 1666, which destroyed the medieval city, it was recognised that thatched roofs presented an unacceptable safety risk and they were banned. Since then, the only building in London to get permission to use thatch was ... Shakespeare's Globe, a modern reconstruction of the old playhouse completed in 1997.

Remarkably, given its unlucky history, Shakespeare's Globe staged *Henry VIII* in 2010. This time, they managed not to burn it down.

27. SHAKESPEARE HAD A BUSY SCHEDULE

When we think about how tightly packed Shakespeare's daily schedule was, it seems amazing that he found any time to write. The life of an Early Modern theatre man was a dizzying round of rehearsals, line learning and, of course, performing. As the chief playwright, a typical day in Shakespeare's life would have been frantic.

The day started early with the whole company being summoned to rehearsals. They were expected to have learnt their lines the evening before. With a young and boisterous company of players, strict rules were needed to keep everybody in line. Infractions such as lateness, drunkenness and unauthorised absence were punishable with fines. So, assuming everybody turned up – on time and not too tipsy – rehearsals could begin. They would rehearse for the entire morning, after which the company would break for dinner. The performance began in the afternoon. We know approximately how long the average play's running time was thanks to the prologue of *Romeo and Juliet* which mentions 'the two hours traffic of our stage'. It was traditional to end a performance with a merry 'jig'. This served to assure the audience that any corpses piled up on stage were not real.

The end of the show did not herald the end of the day's work. As a shareholder and chief playwright, Shakespeare would have spent the evening writing or dealing with paperwork. For the other members of the company, it would have been a long evening learning their lines for the next day – undoubtedly at the local tavern, trying not to get too drunk.

28. He Wrote Thousands of Words but Spoke Only a Few of Them

It is a little-known fact that Shakespeare was also an actor. With a hectic writing schedule it would have been impossible for him to have taken any of the large, juicy roles on offer – we can safely assume he was never a Hamlet or a Romeo – but he made his presence felt on stage in his own subtle, even 'ghostly' way. The first real clue we have to Shakespeare's thespian career comes thanks to that old goat Robert Greene, who, as we saw earlier, referred to him in the *Groatsworth of Wit* as a jack of all trades.

In 1709 Nicholas Rowe edited a compilation of Shakespeare's works. He introduced it with a short 'account of the life of Mr William Shakespeare' in which he asserted that the playwright had acted as 'the ghost in his own *Hamlet*'. He must have been an impressive ghost because Rowe went on to describe him as being 'at the top of his performance'. Rowe was writing from hearsay and crumbs of gossip handed down through the preceding century, but in the absence of any documentary evidence this is all we have. The ghost in *Hamlet* is a fairly small part as is Adam in *As You Like It* who Shakespeare is also said to have played.

If he did indeed play these parts then Shakespeare's few lines on stage included 'Swear' (the ghost) and 'Is 'old dog' my reward? Most true I have lost my teeth in your service' (Adam).

He also played parts in his friend Ben Jonson's plays *Sejanus* and *Every Man in his Humour*.

29. He Wrote Slapstick Comedy for the Groundlings and Highbrow Poetry for the Lords

Whether we like it or not, modern theatre audiences tend to be drawn from a fairly narrow spectrum of society. With ticket prices high, especially in the West End, and a million other forms of cheap entertainment available such as video games, cinema and Netflix, theatre is increasingly a middle-class pastime. It is true that in recent years the industry has tried to reach out to different demographics, with houses such as the National Theatre and Shakespeare's Globe offering some of the most affordable tickets in London, but perhaps decades of complacency has ensured the damage is done. Sadly, many people think Shakespeare is 'not for the likes of them' or 'the language is too hard'. In the 400 years since Shakespeare died a chasm appears to have separated him from his natural audience – ordinary people.

Shakespeare himself had no trouble connecting with people. From apprentices, housewives, prostitutes, fishmongers, apothecaries, knights and earls, everybody wanted a slice of the Shakespeare action. A good proportion of them would have been illiterate and the degree to which they were educated would have varied wildly. So how did Shakespeare ensure that his work maintained a wide appeal? He needed to ensure that everybody who paid their coin had a great time. Whether it was a physician sipping fine wine in the upper gallery, or a ragged groundling shivering in the yard, it was important to retain their custom. Their social status didn't matter a jot.

A popular theory says that Shakespeare tailored his

writing to different elements of the crowd. For instance, his bawdy jokes and prose writing were aimed at the groundlings – those who could not afford a seat in the galleries – while formal blank verse replete with classical allusions was aimed at the lords and ladies and anyone who was educated enough to understand. Of course, the different techniques could just simply be a reflection of the character speaking the words.

Take a look at these two examples from *Henry IV: Part I*:

> So shaken as we are, so wan with care,
> First we a time for frighted peace to pant,
> And breathe short-winded accents of new broils
> To be commenced in strands afar remote,
> *Henry IV: Part I*, Act I, Scene I

The blank verse is formal and rhythmic, as befitting a king. Now see how his reprobate son, Prince Hal, speaks. It is much more naturalistic and closer to how ordinary people speak:

> Thou art so fat-witted, with drinking of old sack and unbuttoning thee after supper and sleeping upon benches after noon, that thou hast forgotten to demand that truly which thou wouldst truly know. What a devil hast thou to do with the time of day?
> Prince Hal, *Henry IV: Part I*, Act I, Scene II

As heir to the throne, Prince Hal is no ordinary person but for as long as he hangs out with wastrels such as Falstaff the fat dissolute knight, Francis the tapster, Poins, Gadshill and Peto, his speech patterns must match theirs.

30. FALSTAFF WAS SO POPULAR THAT SHAKESPEARE FIRED HIM

As well as being rather good at writing, Shakespeare was also interested in the different acting techniques employed by his colleagues. It is fair to say he enjoyed some styles better than others. Let's meet Will Kempe, for instance.

Not much is known about his background, but Kempe managed to leave such a vivid impression on the Elizabethan drama scene that his name is famous as one of the periphery characters in the Shakespeare story. He was a shareholder of the Chamberlain's Men and a very popular comic actor taking on all the clowning roles such as Dogberry in *Much Ado About Nothing*. Such was his natural talent it is said that he only had to poke his head around the side of the stage for the audience to fall about in laughter. Think Morecambe and Wise or Tommy Cooper. Unfortunately for Kempe he was not very good at taking direction or sticking to Shakespeare's carefully crafted lines, preferring to improvise instead. A compelling theory says that Shakespeare and the Chamberlain's Men lost patience with him and threw him out. This happened sometime between the writing of *Henry IV: Part II* and *Henry V*.

How do we know this? The clues come from three plays: *Henry IV: Part II*, *Henry V*, and *Hamlet*. Look at these lines from *Hamlet* first and see who they remind you of:

> ... And let those that play
> Your clowns speak no more than is set down for them;
> For there be of them that will themselves laugh, to
> Set on some quantity of barren spectators to laugh

Too; though, in the meantime, some necessary
Question of the play be then to be considered:
That's villainous, and shows a most pitiful ambition
In the fool that uses it.

Hamlet, Act III, Scene II

This clown sounds very like Will Kempe. *Hamlet* was written after *Henry V*, a play in which the popular clown-like character of Falstaff had been due to feature. Shakespeare had promised as much in the epilogue of *Henry IV: Part II* but the fat knight did not appear. He was killed off in a scene which takes place offstage. The actor is assumed to have been Will Kempe, fired at last for his clumsy clowning. Shortly afterwards, Kempe set off to Norwich. In true clowning style, he morris-danced all the way.

The Chamberlain's Men were not without a clown for long, however. They replaced the undisciplined Kempe with another comic actor. Robert Armin was a different beast to his predecessor. His performances were more subtle and rich. Where Kempe larked around and ad-libbed, Armin was capable of delivering the multi-layered speeches of Shakespeare's later clowns, including Touchstone in *As You Like It* and the Fool in *King Lear*. As a talented singer, he would have been a welcome addition to the team. Shakespeare's fools had to be anything but foolish.

31. He Once Called Himself 'William the Conqueror'

As if it wasn't impressive enough being William Shakespeare!

A hilarious tale dating from 1602 gives an insight into the good natured rivalry which may have been enjoyed between Shakespeare and his fellow actor Richard Burbage. The diarist John Manningham recorded this interesting piece of gossip about their aftershow shenanigans:

> Upon a time when Burbage played Richard III there was a citizen grew so far in liking with him that before she went from the play she appointed him to come that night unto her by the name of Richard the Third. Shakespeare, overhearing their conclusion, went before, was entertained, and at his game ere Burbage came. Their message being brought that Richard the Third was at the door, Shakespeare caused return to be made that William the Conqueror was before Richard the Third.

In case we haven't quite got the joke, Manningham helpfully finishes by reminding us that 'Shakespeare's name (is) William'. The lady in question invited Richard III to her 'aftershow party' but got William the Conqueror instead. She seems not to have minded too much. Maybe she just wanted to bag an actor and any one would do.

It is entirely plausible that groupies were hanging around at the Globe waiting to seduce their favourite stars – after all, the essence of human behaviour doesn't change much – but Manningham's anecdote sounds too neat, too clever to ring entirely true. It is the perfect gag. Richard Burbage was playing his namesake Richard III and as every schoolchild knows, William the Conqueror came before Richard. There is a saucy double entendre in there somewhere ...

32. HE WAS QUITE KEEN ON CROSS-DRESSING

The Shakespearean stage was a riot of transvestism, androgyny, and mistaken identity. No fewer than six of his comedies feature girls dressed as boys meaning that the boy actors had to play girls playing boys. Confused? Let's have a look at some of the cross dressing parts and how they added to the fun:

Viola in *Twelfth Night*: Viola is one of the best loved of Shakespeare's heroines. Witty and resourceful, she finds herself in the middle of a messy love triangle. It begins when Viola finds herself washed up on the shores of Illryia after a shipwreck. She assumes her twin brother Sebastian is dead. Heartbroken, she decides to seek shelter. But as a woman alone on a strange island, her situation is precarious. She persuades the sea captain to help her disguise herself as a man so she can seek work with Orsino, the local nobleman: 'I'll serve this duke: thou shalt present me as an eunuch to him'. Under the name 'Cesario', she becomes Orsino's page and promptly falls in love with him. This is tricky as he thinks she is a man. Orsino meanwhile is in love with Olivia and sends 'Cesario' off to court her on his behalf. Things get really complicated when Olivia falls in love with 'Cesario' not realising that 'he' is a 'she'.

Rosalind in *As You Like It*: Rosalind has been living under the protection of her uncle Duke Frederick who has exiled her father and usurped his lands. Her best friend is her cousin Celia with whom she spends all her time. One day, the Duke takes a dislike to Rosalind. He calls her a traitor and exiles her too. As best mates Rosalind and Celia decide to stick together and flee into the forest. The only trouble is, it might be dangerous for two women to go off together unprotected, so, in true Shakespearean style, Rosalind dresses as a man: 'Were it not better, because that I am more than common tall, that I did suit me all points like a man? A gallant curtle axe upon my thigh, a boar spear in my hand'. In their guises as Ganymede and Aliena, Rosalind and Celia travel deep into the Forest of Arden where they encounter another recent exile, the handsome Orlando. Rosalind is already in love with him, having spotted him at court, but – oops! – she is dressed as a man.

Jessica in *The Merchant of Venice*: Jessica's tale is more straightforward. The daughter of Shylock, she begins a forbidden love affair with Lorenzo and elopes with him disguised as a boy. Despite her eagerness to run away, she does not seem altogether comfortable in her male attire when Lorenzo comes to meet her: 'I am glad 'tis night, you do not look on me, for I am much ashamed of my exchange ... Cupid himself would blush to see me thus transformed to a boy.'

In *The Merry Wives of Windsor* the old rogue Falstaff is persuaded to dress as a woman. It was the nascent spirit of pantomime.

33. The Obscure Play *Edward III* Contains a Passage Written by Shakespeare

The First Folio of Mr William Shakespeare's Comedies, Histories and Tragedies contains thirty-six plays attributed to the great man, yet it may not be a complete catalogue of his endeavours.

In 1596 the printer Cuthbert Burby published an anonymous play, presumably to be sold at St Paul's Churchyard like every other piece of printed work. The author was anonymous. There was no star billing this time; no Mr W. Shakespeare proudly emblazoned on the front cover. The play was called *The Reign of Edward the Third* and, according to the title page, this first quarto was a complete version of the play 'as it hath been sundrie times plaid about the Citie of London'.

The first half of the play tells the story of Edward III's battle with the rebellious Scots. They are besieging a castle in the north of England, so Edward races up there to rescue the distressed chatelaine, the Countess of Salisbury. After chasing the invaders away he finds time for a spot of seduction and attempts to woo the countess. She resists his advances and threatens to kill herself if he does not leave her alone. Chastened, he resolves to become a better person and rule his kingdom wisely. With that, he rides off to France in an attempt to seize the French crown, believing himself to be the rightful heir. After a few skirmishes on the battlefield Edward captures Calais and they all live happily ever after, with the notable exception of the French king, of course. He has lost everything.

It is a patchy play with an inconsistent style. Scholars

believe the bulk of it was written by Thomas Kyd, a playwright who had died two years prior to its publication. Kyd was a roommate of the controversial playwright Christopher Marlowe and suffered greatly for the association. Government agents searched their lodgings and found atheist tracts belonging to Marlowe. They arrested Kyd for interrogation and left him to rot in prison for the rest of the year; he died shortly after his release. Kyd is remembered as the author of *The Spanish Tragedy* and the so called *Ur-Hamlet*, believed to be a forerunner of Shakespeare's play.

It is likely that Kyd collaborated with Shakespeare on *Edward III*. Some scholars attribute Edward's unsuccessful wooing of the Countess of Salisbury to Shakespeare, asserting that the style bears his mark. Judge for yourself:

> King Edward: It is thy beauty that I would enjoy.
> Countess: O, were it painted, I would wipe it off
> And dispossess myself, to give it thee.
> But, sovereign, it is soldered to my life:
> Take one and take both; for like an humble shadow,
> It haunts the sunshine of my summer's life.
> *Edward III* Act I, Scene II

If this is Shakespeare's writing the mystery is why the play was excluded from the First Folio. Perhaps it was the wisest thing to do, considering that England was now ruled by a Scottish king and the play was not very flattering to England's northern cousins.

34. Shakespeare Was the Love Child of Elizabeth I – Sort Of

In 1594, when *Edward III* was written, any worries about offending King James lay far off in the future. For now, the only person Shakespeare had to worry about was Queen Elizabeth I. The daughter of Anne Boleyn and Henry VIII, Elizabeth had been on the throne for a whopping thirty-six years, making her the longest reigning monarch in living memory. Indeed, for someone of Shakespeare's generation, Elizabeth was the only figurehead they had ever known.

We have come to think of the Elizabethan era as the 'Golden Age': a period in which England saw a flowering of Renaissance ideas. In every field of human endeavour – literature, music, theatre, art, science and exploration – the youth of England was ablaze with creative energy. Under Elizabeth's watchful gaze, Francis Drake circumnavigated the globe, Sir Walter Raleigh sailed to the Indies and discovered tobacco, William Byrd composed sacred music, Sir John Harrington invented the flushing toilet, Nicholas Hilliard painted his exquisite miniature portraits, and Shakespeare revolutionised the English language. What was it about Elizabeth's reign that made the age such a fertile breeding ground of ideas? Perhaps it was part of England's progression from a Catholic to an Anglican state; a career in the church was no longer the only option. Minds began to focus on more worldly matters.

Elizabeth herself was in the business of invention. As a queen without a consort she nurtured an image of Gloriana, the virgin queen married to her country. She was not without suitors. Foreign princes from the Duke of Anjou to Erik of Sweden tried to win her hand. There was also interest from gentlemen at home, including Robert Dudley, the Earl of Leicester. Elizabeth died intact but that has not stopped speculation about her supposed love life and her secret babies.

Shakespeare himself has been linked to the queen. A theory proposed by the author Paul Streitz suggests that Shakespeare was not the son of Mary Arden and John Shakespeare of Warwickshire but the son of Queen Elizabeth I. (No sniggering at the back!) According to Streitz, his father was Thomas Seymour, brother to the late Jane Seymour who died after giving birth to Henry VIII's only son, Edward VI. Young Shakespeare was raised as the same Edward de Vere, Earl of Oxford, who – of course – went on to write the plays. The authorship question has been dealt with in a previous chapter so we won't dwell any further on that, and the theory that Shakespeare was Elizabeth's son is too ludicrous to contemplate. It is true that when Elizabeth was an adolescent Thomas Seymour entered her bedroom and played dubious 'tickling games' with her but it does not follow that they slept together, much less that she bore a child who went on to write Shakespeare. If Shakespeare was Elizabeth's love child, he was not a product of her loins but instead of the creative environment she nurtured. That's the plain old boring truth. Having said that, Prince Shakespeare does have a certain ring to it ...

35. A MIDSUMMER NIGHT'S DREAM WAS WRITTEN FOR A WEDDING

We cannot claim that Shakespeare was the love child of Elizabeth I but there was plenty of other comedy during her reign. In fact, out of all his fourteen comedies only one of them – *All's Well that Ends Well* – was written during the Jacobean phase of his career. One of the most magical and side splitting Elizabethan era comedies is *A Midsummer Night's Dream*, with its cast of fairies, mischievous sprites and bickering young lovers. The action takes place in a forest outside Athens and, in similar strain to *As You Like It*, features a gang of young runaways.

Briefly, the plot goes like this: Hermia's father has ordered her to marry Demetrius but she is in love with Lysander so refuses to obey. Under threat of execution, she and her sweetheart elope into the forest in search of the home of Lysander's aunt, where they hope to marry. Meanwhile, Demetrius is hot in pursuit of his runaway bride. Tagging along with him is Helena, the woman he spurned for Hermia. Helena still loves him. As this quartet of ill-starred youngsters stumble around in the forest, Theseus, the Duke of Athens, is preparing to marry Hippolyta, the Queen of the Amazons. They commission a band of 'rude mechanicals' to prepare a play for the wedding entertainments. Much hilarity ensues as Bottom, Flute, Starveling and pals rehearse their lines. The young lovers in the wood are eventually reconciled with the help of some magic fairy juice and a group wedding.

With so much love in the air, it would appear that Shakespeare had a special event in mind when he wrote it – perhaps a real-life wedding.

The play is usually dated to around 1595 and was 'sundry times publickly acted' by the Chamberlain's Men according to the title page of the first quarto. It was obviously a hit at the public playhouses, but most scholars agree it had been specially commissioned for an aristocratic wedding. It just so happens that around this time, Henry Carey, the Lord Chamberlain – Shakespeare's patron – was preparing for the marriage of his granddaughter Elizabeth who was about to marry Sir Thomas Berkeley. The marriage took place on 19 February 1596, probably in the fashionable Blackfriars area where the Carey family kept a grand residence. The post-nuptial entertainments would have been lavish with no expense spared, the evening a whirl of masques, dances and games. It seems obvious that the Lord Chamberlain would make full use of his company of players in honour of Elizabeth's wedding. Imagine the great hall as Shakespeare and friends took to the stage, their painted faces glowing in the flickering candlelight. Hermia and Helena were boys in dresses but disbelief was suspended as the wedding party settled down to enjoy the show. Imagine their laughter in Act I, Scene II as they heard the actor playing Flute exclaim: 'Nay, faith, let me not play a woman; I have a beard coming.'

It would have been a joyful occasion.

36. Shakespeare Had His Haters

Not everybody was a fan of *A Midsummer Night's Dream*. Nearly seventy years after that magical evening in Blackfriars, the diarist Samuel Pepys went to see the play at the King's Theatre on Vere Street. He didn't like it. On Monday 29 September 1662 he wrote: 'We saw A 'Midsummer Night's Dream' which I had never seen before, nor shall ever again, for it is the most insipid ridiculous play that I ever saw in my life. I saw, I confess, some good dancing and some handsome women, which was all my pleasure.'

Trust randy old Pepys to notice the 'handsome women'! Nevertheless he reminds us that Shakespeare has not always been universally idolised over the centuries and in fact has had no shortage of haters. Here are some of them – boo, hiss!

Lord Byron: The Romantic poet composed this evisceration of Shakespeare in a letter he wrote to James Hogg in 1814. Although he has a good point about Shakespeare's lack of originality when it came to his plots, he misses the point. Shakespeare is admired for his language, not his storylines. 'Shakespeare's name, you may depend upon it, stands absurdly too high, and will go down. He had no invention as to stories, none whatever. He took all his plots from old novels and threw their stories into a dramatic shape ... As for his historical plays, properly historical, I mean, they were mere re-dressings of former plays on the same subjects.'

Tolstoy: The Russian novelist Leo Tolstoy was repulsed by Shakespeare. Writing in 1906 he said, 'I remember the astonishment I felt when I first read Shakespeare. I expected to receive a powerful aesthetic pleasure, but having read, one after the other, works regarded as his best: *King Lear*, *Romeo and Juliet*, *Hamlet*, and *Macbeth*, not only did I feel no delight, but I felt an irresistible repulsion and tedium.' No doubt generations of reluctant schoolchildren would sympathise with these sentiments but Tolstoy was reading the plays in Russian – you have to wonder whether any of Shakespeare's soaring poetry had been lost in translation.

Charles Darwin: 'I have tried lately to read Shakespeare and found it so intolerably dull that it nauseated me.' To be fair to the great evolutionary scientist, he was trying to explain how he had lost his taste for the arts lately, despite having loved paintings and poetry in his youth. He wasn't just picking on Shakespeare.

George Bernard Shaw: The same cannot be said for Bernard Shaw who genuinely hated the Bard: 'There is no eminent writer, not even Sir Walter Scott, whom I despise so entirely as I despise Shakespeare ... It would be positively a relief to me to dig him up and throw stones at him.' He also complained about the 'emptiness of Shakespeare's philosophy' and his 'weakness and incoherence as a thinker'.

Let's agree to disagree, George.

37. The Bloodiest Play in the Canon Is *Titus Andronicus* in Which Fourteen Characters Die Horribly

One of Shakespeare's earliest plays was also his bloodiest. The gore-spattered tragedy of *Titus Andronicus* is thought to have been written sometime between 1588 and 1593, making it Shakespeare's first attempt at tragedy. It is a story of unquenchable bloodlust and revenge. Titus Andronicus returns victorious from a war against the Goths, bringing with him some prisoners including the Goth queen Tamora and her sons. In the absence of anything like the Geneva Convention, Titus kills one of Tamora's sons and sets off a train of events that culminates in half the characters being murdered in inventively macabre ways.

When the play was staged at Shakespeare's Globe in 2006 and 2014, many audience members fainted or left the theatre in shock. Those with a weak stomach may wish to look away now as we run through some of the grisly deaths and mutilations:

Alarbus: One of Tamora's sons and her fellow prisoner of war, Titus picks him out for sacrifice upon his triumphant return to Rome. Alarbus is 'the proudest prisoner of the Goths' so Titus orders his men to take him away and 'hew his limbs til they be clean consumed'. In language reminiscent of the Elizabethan executioner, the murderers report that his 'entrails feed the sacrificing fire'.

Lavinia: In another unsettling scene Titus's daughter Lavinia is carried into the forest and raped. The attackers are Demetrius and Chiron who cut out her tongue and remove her hands to stop her from naming them.

Titus: Lavinia is not the only one to suffer a mutilation. Tamora's lover Aaron falsely accuses Titus's sons Martius and Quintus of the attack on Lavinia. He tells Titus that if he sends him the severed hand of either himself or his other son Lucius, then Martius and Quintus will be spared execution. Titus duly allows Aaron to cut off his hand but he has been tricked – the severed heads of Martius and Quintus arrive in the post shortly afterwards.

Demetrius and Chiron: Lavinia's attackers do not escape scot-free. Titus slits their throats and drains their blood into a basin which his daughter helpfully holds out for him. Titus then bakes them in a pie.

Lavinia: Having already suffered a rape and mutilation at the hands of Demetrius and Chiron, Lavinia's troubles are not over yet. Titus asks his friend Saturninus for advice on whether a 'deflowered' daughter should be killed. Saturninus thinks it would be a good idea because 'the girl should not survive her shame'. Titus kills Lavinia with the words, 'Die, die, Lavinia, and thy shame with thee.'

Titus: Having killed his daughter, Titus tells Tamora that her sons are baked in the pie she has just been eating. He then kills her and is in turn swiftly killed by Saturninus.

Titus Andronicus was first performed in 1594 at The Rose playhouse on Bankside. It was an area characterised by the blood sports on offer; bull-baiting, bear-baiting and cockfighting were all on the menu – the perfect location for such a grim tragedy.

38. *The Merchant of Venice* Was an Audacious Rebuttal to Contemporary Prejudice Against Jews

It was not much fun living in the Elizabethan era if you were in any way different. It was especially hard if you happened to be a Jew, as they were not even supposed to be in the country. It was Edward I who expelled all the Jews from England back in 1290, and the edict had never been rescinded. That is not to say there were no Jews in England; in fact Shakespeare himself would have been very aware of one in particular. Doctor Roderigo Lopez was a Portuguese national. He moved to England where he became a physician of distinction and renown. The first-ever doctor to work at St Bartholomew's hospital in Smithfield, in time Lopez became Elizabeth's own personal physician. Not bad for a foreigner in a xenophobic age. Things went wrong for him in 1594 when he was accused of trying to kill the queen. He was placed on trial at the Guildhall in London, found guilty and then taken to Smithfield where he was hanged, drawn and quartered. It was a controversial case. Lopez was widely believed to have been fitted up. His accuser, Robert Devereaux, the Earl of Essex had taken a dislike to him and pursued a case against him, alleging that the doctor was conspiring with Catholic Spain against Her Majesty. At first the queen did not believe a word of it. She trusted Lopez and had no reason to believe that he would wish her harm.

The unfortunate doctor confessed to the plot after being threatened with torture but later retracted his statement claiming it had been made under duress. After his death Elizabeth felt so remorseful that she paid a pension to Lopez's widow by way of reparation.

The following year, Shakespeare and his company, the Chamberlain's Men, presented a new play, *The Merchant of Venice*. It told the story of a Jew, Shylock, who lends money to the merchant Antonio, on the condition that if the sum is not repaid in full by a certain time he will take a pound of the merchant's flesh. On the face of it this was a hideous portrayal of the stereotypical 'grasping Jew' of popular culture.

But Shakespeare was not interested in one dimensional caricatures. He gave Shylock some of the most moving lines in the entire canon; an attempt perhaps to remind his audience that Jews, too, were human:

> Hath not a Jew eyes?
> Hath not a Jew hands, organs,
> Dimensions, senses, affections, passions? Fed with
> The same food, hurt with the same weapons, subject
> To the same diseases, healed by the same means,
> Warmed and cooled by the same winter and summer, as
> A Christian is? If you prick us do we not bleed?
> Shylock, *The Merchant of Venice,* Act III, Scene I

It was a departure from previous portrayals of Jews at the playhouse. In 1592, Christopher Marlowe's *Jew of Malta* had shocked and alarmed audiences with the antics of the villainous Jew Barabas, a Machiavellian character who murders his way to power. Marlowe confirmed his audience's prejudices. Shakespeare preferred to challenge them.

39. FALSTAFF WAS ELIZABETH I'S FAVOURITE SHAKESPEAREAN CHARACTER

As we saw earlier, the character of Falstaff was one of Shakespeare's favourites. He appeared in both parts of *Henry IV* as a hard-drinking ne'er-do-well who wastes his days drinking in taverns and getting into scrapes. He is an imperfect human being but, despite all his faults, he is also one of the most lovable in Shakespeare. According to some he was a big hit with Elizabeth I, who demanded that Shakespeare resurrect the character in a new play. Two uncorroborated sources from the eighteenth century tell the story, the first from the dramatist John Dennis, writing in 1702: 'I know very well that it hath pleased one of the greatest queens that ever one in the world ... This comedy was written at her command, and by her direction, and she was so eager to see it acted that she commanded it to be finished in fourteen days; and was afterwards, as tradition tells us, very well pleased at the representation.'

Where he got the story from is unknown, but a few years later, Nicholas Rowe added some more detail to it. He writes that the queen 'was so well pleased with that admirable character of Falstaff in the two parts of *Henry IV* that she commanded him to continue it for one play more, and to show him in love'. Again, it would be interesting to know where Rowe got this information from. After all, he was writing nearly a century after Shakespeare had died. It is a nice story though – and could well be true.

40. *The Merry Wives of Windsor* Is the Only Shakespeare Play in a Contemporary English Setting

Although many of Shakespeare's plays are at least partly set in Britain – the history plays making up the bulk of them – he shied away from setting the action in what anyone would recognise as Tudor England. This made good political sense, for who would wish to risk an accusation of writing about the affairs of the great and the good? Writers were routinely jailed for causing offence, as Ben Jonson learned to his cost in 1605 when he poked fun at the Scots in *Eastward Ho*, a play which the new Scottish king James I found extremely unfunny.

If it is true that *The Merry Wives of Windsor* was commissioned by Elizabeth I then Shakespeare would have been able to write with confidence, aware that what was wanted was a fine comedy laced with a good deal of flattery. This was not the time for biting satire.

As the title suggests, the play was set in Windsor, a handsome town outside London on the River Thames. It is easy to see why he chose this location as Windsor just so happened to boast a royal castle, the imposing fortress which dominates the skyline. Windsor Castle was established by William the Conqueror who invaded England in 1066. To consolidate his grip on power he began building protective fortresses to repel invaders. The Tower of London is the most famous example, with Windsor Castle serving to protect the capital from invasion from the west. By Shakespeare's day, the castle had been enlarged to the extent that its looming presence over the town of Windsor was as impressive as it is today.

One of the main attractions for tourists today is St George's Chapel, the mother church of the Order of the Garter, which hosted the St George's Day ceremony in which new members were created. It was an illustrious order and only those closest to the queen were given the honour of joining its ranks. Around 1598 or 1599, when Shakespeare is believed to have written *The Merry Wives of Windsor*, recent appointees to the order were Sir Henry Lee and Henry Brooke, 8th Earl of Cobham. There are several references in the play to both the castle and the Order of the Garter, making it even more likely that Shakespeare was aiming this directly at the queen. For example, in Act V when Mistress Quickly tries to frighten Falstaff with a scary song:

> About, about,
> Search Windsor Castle, elves, within and without:
> Strew good luck, ouphs, on every room:
> That it may stand til the perpetual doom,
> In state as wholesome as in state 'tis fit,
> Worthy the owner, and the owner it.

The owner of course was Elizabeth I, who may have listened to these lines with nodding approval. Mistress Quickly continues with a reference to the Order of the Garter:

> More fertile fresh than all the field to see;
> And 'Honi soit qui mal y pense' write ...

Honi soit qui mal y pense is the motto of the order; Shakespeare certainly knew his audience.

41. DESPITE WRITING AROUND THIRTY-SEVEN PLAYS HE ONLY CAME UP WITH FOUR ORIGINAL PLOTLINES

We saw earlier how Shakespeare has often been criticised over the years for his lack of originality when it came to thinking up storylines. He may have been the greatest poet in the history of English playwrights, but let's face it, he lifted most of his storylines from others.

Here are the four storylines which Shakespeare dreamt up by himself:

The Merry Wives of Windsor: Falstaff plans to seduce two of the local ladies, Mistress Page and Mistress Ford, in order to fleece them of their money. He is thwarted when the ladies compare notes and realise what he is up to. The wily wives of Windsor devise a public shaming to teach Falstaff a lesson.

Love's Labour's Lost: Ferdinand, the King of Navarre and his companions Berowne, Dumaine and Longaville have sworn to give up women and spend their time in sober study. Their resolve is tested when a beautiful princess and her entourage of ladies comes to visit.

A Midsummer Night's Dream: Forbidden lovers Hermia and Lysander elope to the woods, closely followed by Demetrius and his admirer Helena. Demetrius is in love with Hermia and Helena is in love with Demetrius. Things get even more confusing when a sprite names Puck begins smearing magic juice over everyone.

The Tempest: A shipwreck strands Ferdinand and his companions on a magical island haunted by Ariel, Caliban, the magician Prospero and his daughter Miranda. Ferdinand and Miranda fall in love. Prospero imprisons Ferdinand to slow the affair down a bit while Antonio and Sebastian plan a spot of murder.

With no recognised sources, it seems that all of these plays came directly from Shakespeare's imagination, proving that he could invent stories when he felt like it. His sources for the history plays – *Richard II, Richard III, Henry IV* (parts I and II), *Henry V, Henry VI* (parts I, II and III), and *Henry VIII* – came from Holinshead's *Chronicles of England Scotland and Ireland* plus Edward Hall's *Union of the Two Noble and Illustre Families of Lancaster and York*. For the comedies and tragedies, Shakespeare drew upon a range of classical sources. Looking at the following examples, it is hard to imagine how anyone could possibly call Shakespeare an uneducated hick from Stratford Grammar:

King Lear: In 1605, shortly before Shakespeare wrote this family tragedy, he may have got hold of the recently published text of *The True Chronicle of King Leir,* a play which had been performed ten years previously. Lines from Edmund Spenser's *The Faerie Queen* also deal with the mythical British king and his daughter troubles.

Julius Caesar: In dramatising Caesar's murder and the events which followed, Shakespeare was indebted to North's translation of Plutarch.

The Comedy of Errors: This comedy of mistaken identity was lifted straight from *The Menaechmi*, a play by Plautus. Shakespeare embellished and perfected the story. He would have read the play in its original Latin as the first translation did not appear until after *The Comedy of Errors* had been written.

42. The Shakespeare Canon Contains about 18,000 Words ...

... Many of which are some of the most inventive insults known to man. Shakespeare must have had enormous fun coming up with these brilliant put-downs. In honour of the great insulter himself, here are some of his best diatribes all rolled into one:

A bawling, blasphemous, incharitable dog. An asshead, and a coxcomb, and a knave, a thin faced knave, a gull! A base football player. A whoreson impudent embossed rascal. Thou damned tripe-visaged rascal; thou paper-faced villain. Thou art a toad; ugly and venomous. Thou art a flesh-monger, a fool and a coward. Thy tongue out-venoms all the worms of Nile. You scullion. You rampallion. You fustilarian. I'll tickle your catastrophe. Thou art a base, proud, shallow, beggarly, three-suited, hundred-pound, filthy worsted stocking knave; a lily livered, action taking, whoreson, glass-gazing, superserviceable, finical rogue; one-trunk-inheriting slave; one that wouldst be a bawd in way of good service, and art nothing but the composition of a knave, beggar, coward, pandar, and the son and heir of a mongrel bitch; one who I will beat into clamorous whining if thou deniest the least syllable of thy addition.

Don't take it personally!

It is impossible to deny the power of his invention. Shakespeare is also celebrated for coining brand new words and adding to the richness of the English language. The Oxford English Dictionary attributes the first cited used of the following words to Shakespeare:

Bloodsucking, blusterer, braggartism, brisky, castigate, circumstantial, countless, critical, cruelhearted, dauntless, denote, dewdrop, dishearten, dislocate, engagement, exposure, fairyland, fitful, footfall, full-grown, gentlefolk, grovel, hostile, inauspicious, inaudible, ladybird.

43. Shakespeare Thought Henry VII Was Boring

Shakespeare's history plays cover the dramatic story of the Wars of the Roses in which the two warring sides, Lancaster and York, battled for the crown of England. He dedicated entire plays to the main actors Henry VI and Richard III but had nothing to say about the ultimate victor Henry VII. Why was this? After all, it would have been flattering to Elizabeth I to portray her grandfather's triumph on the public stage, a brilliant opportunity to carry out some Tudor propaganda and earn some brownie points.

There are three possible reasons why he neglected the founder of the Tudor dynasty, the first of which hinges on the premise that Shakespeare did not do propaganda. Or if he ever strayed into that territory, he was careful not to lie. Fans of the hunchbacked king Richard III would disagree with this. They would argue that Shakespeare's unflattering portrayal of Richard was pure propaganda, a deliberate attempt to blacken his name whilst bolstering the claim of his Tudor queen. Until Richard was disinterred from his resting place beneath a car park in Leicester, his defenders had accused Shakespeare of inventing a malformed villain in keeping with the Tudor belief that a twisted spine signified a twisted soul. Scientists discovered that Richard did indeed have curvature of the spine, or scoliosis, vindicating Shakespeare. He had merely written the truth.

The second possible reason for omitting Henry VII is that the victorious king had already featured quite heavily in the play *Richard III*.

Appearing in his previous incarnation as the 2nd

Earl of Richmond, Henry is shown as the force of good against evil. He is an unflashy, level-headed foil to the Machiavellian Richard, leading his troops into battle without fuss. By contrast, Richard is plagued with nightmares as his conscience torments him for the crimes he has committed. The ghosts of his victims – Anthony Rivers, Clarence, and the two princes murdered in the Tower of London – visit Richard on the eve of the Battle of Bosworth. They rain curses upon him before blessing the sleeping form of Henry Tudor. For the Tudors, there was no doubt whose side Shakespeare was on. Henry Tudor had been portrayed as just and fair – the rightful victor in a war which had torn England apart. Perhaps Shakespeare thought Henry had had his day in the sun and there was no reason to write anything more about him.

The third and probably most compelling reason for Henry VII not to have a play of his own is that he was actually quite dull. Reigning from 1485 until his death in 1509, Henry's rule was characterised by the twin virtues of care and thrift. He kept a close eye on the nation's finances, slowly building up the wealth of the crown by raising taxes and not spending very much. There would be no swashbuckling into war or lurid love affairs. He left that to his flamboyant son Henry VIII.

Shakespeare simply had nothing to say about him.

44. The War of the Poets Was His Very Own War of the Roses

It was one thing to write about the historical Wars of the Roses but for the first couple of years of the seventeenth-century Shakespeare was involved in a war of his own. It was called the War of the Poets or, sometimes, the War of the Theatres. No blood was shed but delicate egos were wounded and reputations libelled.

This 'luvvie's tiff' started in 1599 when the playwright John Marston wrote his catchily titled play *Histriomastix*. Translated into English the title means *The Player Whipped*. Whether or not Marston had actually been fantasising about whipping his playhouse colleagues it seems he was in the mood for an argument. One of his characters was the unlikeable Chrisoganus, a proud arrogant figure who was mocked throughout the drama. Unfortunately Chrisoganus happened to remind audiences of someone they knew. This someone was Marston's rival playwright Ben Jonson. The first shot had been fired in a spat which would last until 1602.

Jonson was quick to retaliate. How dare anyone call him proud! Furious, he dashed out his response in the play *Every Man in his Humour*, which contained mocking references to Marston's fustian, verbose style. *Every Man* was performed by the Chamberlain's Men with Shakespeare in one of the roles, although we do not know which one. Marston and Jonson batted plays back and forth at one another in similar vein until 1601 when Thomas Dekker joined in the fun. The character Horace in Dekker's play *Satiromastix* was a thinly veiled attack on Jonson, presenting the rival playwright as an arrogant hypocrite.

So what was going on here? Why did these playwrights suddenly start having digs at one another? There are several theories in circulation, one of which sees the 'War' as little more than a bunch of writers showing off. Marston and Jonson were writing for rival companies of child actors and were in competition for audiences, so perhaps that explains why they went through this period of belittling each other on stage. Another theory muses on the possibility that it was all a publicity stunt to provoke more interest in what was happening on stage, thus increasing bums on seats.

The fact that the insults were being hurled about by men writing for children's companies makes some scholars think that a passage in *Hamlet* was inspired by the War of the Poets. In this scene Hamlet, Rosencrantz and Guildenstern have been chatting about the strange phenomenon of child actors. Rosencrantz tells Hamlet that they have caused upset in the theatre industry:

Rosencrantz: Faith, there has been much to do on both sides; and the nation holds it no sin to tar them to controversy: there was, for a while, no money bid for argument unless the poet and the player went to cuffs in the question.
Hamlet: Is't possible?
Guildenstern: O, there has been much throwing about of brains.

Hamlet, Act II, Scene II

There was much throwing about of brains in Shakespeare's work, full stop. As we shall see, he quite enjoyed killing off his characters.

45. THERE ARE THIRTEEN SUICIDES IN SHAKESPEARE – UNLUCKY FOR SOME

The number thirteen is considered to be bad news – so much so that even hotel rooms have been known to jump straight from number twelve to number fourteen, leaving out that unlucky number altogether. In numerology the number thirteen is associated with destruction and upheaval, so it may be no coincidence that it also represents the number of suicides in Shakespeare. Here is a rundown of the unlucky few and the fate that befalls them:

Romeo: The tragic hero of Shakespeare's greatest romance is in despair. He has been told that his sweetheart Juliet is dead. There is nothing else for it – he must join her in death. He goes to the Capulet crypt where Juliet lies, buying some poison on the way. Lying down beside her, he drinks the poison and dies.

Juliet: What a shame Romeo did not get the message that Juliet was only pretending to be dead! In her attempt to avoid marriage to Paris, she has taken a potion that puts her into a deep sleep, fooling everybody that she is dead. Lying in the crypt, the drug wears off and she discovers that Romeo has killed himself. With none of the poison left, she stabs herself with his dagger.

Lady Macbeth: The scheming wife of Macbeth falls into madness after her part in the murder of King Duncan. She dies offstage with a scream and Macbeth is told that she is dead. We never find out exactly how she died but it is assumed that it was by her own hand.

Antony: Fearing that Cleopatra has killed herself, Antony attempts to run himself through with a sword only to discover that Cleopatra is still alive. Severely wounded, he dies.

Cleopatra: Captured by Caesar and threatened with being paraded to Rome before the mocking gaze of the crowds, the Egyptian queen dresses in her finest gown then sends for a basket of asps. She presses one to her breast and one to her arm, allowing them to sink their fangs into her flesh.

Charmian: Wishing to join her mistress in death, Charmian also commits suicide by asp.

Brutus: Runs himself through with his sword after losing a battle.

Cassius: In grief at the death of his friend Titinius, Cassius asks his servant to kill him. This also avoids the possibility that he will be killed in battle.

Portia: Commits suicide because her husband Brutus is away from home too often.

Timon: After retiring to a cave in the woods, Timon refuses to come back to Athens and civilisation. He dies in the wilderness.

Othello: After killing his wife Desdemona in a jealous rage, Othello stabs himself to death.

Ophelia: Drowns in a brook. The sexton alleges it was suicide.

Goneril: One of the evil sisters in *King Lear*, Goneril discovers that her sister has an eye for Edmund. This will not do as Goneril is also in love with him, so she poisons her sister and then kills herself offstage.

46. There Is Only One Surviving Letter to Shakespeare – And He May Not Even Have Seen It

Shakespeare was doing very well for himself in London. He had established a successful career with the Chamberlain's Men and was growing steadily richer with each passing year. It was a far cry from the days when he was little more than a young glover's son from Stratford. His home town, by contrast, was not doing so well. The year 1598 saw Stratford suffer a series of disasters which almost brought the pretty little market town to its knees. The River Avon burst its banks, causing floods and harvest failure. If this was not bad enough, there was the fire which ripped through the timber fabric of the town destroying homes and businesses alike. The devastating impact on the local economy cannot be underestimated. 1598 was an *annus horribilis* indeed.

On top of this the crown was demanding its taxes from Stratford, a town which could barely afford to feed itself let alone contribute to the royal coffers. With this in mind Richard Quiney, a friend of Shakespeare, travelled down to London to plead for respite. Whilst in the capital, Quiney lodged near St Paul's Cathedral at the Bell Inn on Carter Lane. He stayed there for four months, during which time his own personal finances began to suffer. It was at this point that he seems to have remembered his wealthy friend, the famous William Shakespeare. Quiney wrote him a letter:

> Loving countryman, I am bold of you as a friend, craving your help with thirty pounds ... you shall friend me much in helping me out of all the debts I

owe in London, I thank God, and much quiet my mind which would not be indebted. I am now toward the court in hope of answer for the dispatch of my business ... You shall neither lose credit nor money by me, the Lord willing, and now but persuade yourself, so as I hope, and you shall not need to fear but with all hearty thankfulness I will hold my time.

The tone of Quiney's letter suggests a man who was frantic with worry, as well he might be. A debtor could be thrown in gaol until he paid his dues, but Quiney was keen to assure his friend that he would get the money back. The letter was found among Quiney's belongings after his death in 1602 meaning that, for whatever reason, he chose not to send it. Perhaps he bumped into Shakespeare in the teeming streets of Elizabethan London and made his request in person. The Globe was just on the other side of the River Thames from Carter Lane so it would have been easy for Quiney to hail a wherry boat and visit his friend at the playhouse.

The other possibility is that he changed his mind about asking Shakespeare. After all, there are some lines in *Hamlet*, a play Shakespeare may have been writing at the time, which could give a clue as to the likely outcome of such a request: *Neither a borrower nor a lender be.*

47. He Was 'Not Without Mustard'

We twenty-first-century folk like to think of ourselves as living in a classless society in which anyone, no matter how obscure their roots, can rise to the very top of the Establishment. It was different in Shakespeare's day, to say the least. Elizabethans were so hot on status that Shakespeare even wrote about it in one of his plays. In *Troilus and Cressida*, the character Ulysses expounds upon the importance of everyone knowing their place. An ordered society could only be maintained if everybody knew where they stood in the pecking order. As Ulysses says: 'Take but degree away, untune that spring, and hark, what discord follows!' Despite Ulysses' warning, people still strove to change their 'degree' and improve their ranking in society. Shakespeare and his father John certainly had a go, with varying degrees of success.

In 1568, John Shakespeare, as High Bailiff of Stratford, decided it was high time he had a coat of arms. He put in an application to the heralds at the College of Arms in London with supporting evidence as to why he should be granted such a great honour. John claimed that his great-grandfather had done 'faithful and approved service' to Henry VII. We don't know the nature of this service but it is likely to have been military. Applying for a coat of arms was an expensive business – the heralds needed to be paid for their time in researching the family history and verifying the information provided by the applicant. It is possibly for this reason that John Shakespeare did not continue with the process and let the matter drop. Nearly thirty years later, his son William Shakespeare revived the claim on his behalf. This time the Shakespeares were in a more fortunate position, what with William's new-found wealth. They were rewarded in 1596 when they were finally awarded their coat of arms. It was a yellow shield shot through diagonally by a black banner and silver spear signifying the second syllable in the Shakespeare name. Shake – spear, geddit? Along with the coat of arms came the right to call themselves gentlemen. They chose the motto 'Non sanz droict', meaning 'not without right'. It was a defensive statement to anyone who might disapprove. So Shakespeare had certainly improved his 'degree' but not everybody was pleased for him.

Our old friend Ben Jonson, he of the 'Poet's War', dug out his quill and went on the attack one more. This time he may have had his tongue firmly in cheek but it was a definite barb. In 1599 he wrote the follow-up to *Every Man in His Humour* with *Every Man Out of His Humour*. Ben Jonson was certainly out of humour, making a pointed reference to Shakespeare's rise in fortune, misquoting his motto as 'Not without mustard.' He goes on to mock: 'I' faith I thank God I can write myself a gentle man now; here's my patent, it cost me thirty pound, by this breath.'

48. *King John* is Our Least Favourite Shakespeare Play

Even literary geniuses such as William Shakespeare sometimes have their off-key moments. The play King *John* is officially our least favourite in the entire Shakespeare canon, for reasons which shall become evident. Written around the same time as Shakespeare was applying for his coat of arms, it is a difficult play to love. Perhaps the Bard had his mind on other things.

Shining a light on the thorny issue of royal legitimacy, *King John* tells the story of England's most villainous monarch. In comparison to Shakespeare's other history plays the pace of *King John* is slower and more ponderous. This being Shakespeare, it has its flashes of poetic brilliance, for example in these lines from Act III, Scene IV when Constance grieves over her dead son:

> Grief fills up the room of my absent child,
> Lies in his bed, walks up and down with me,
> Puts on his pretty looks, repeats his words,
> Remembers me of all his gracious parts,
> Stuffs out his vacant garments with his form ...

These gorgeous lines are the highlight of the whole play, the remainder being a fairly tedious trudge through issues of succession and inheritance. Consequently it is performed very rarely. Two pioneering theatre companies have stepped up to the challenge in recent years, however. The Royal Shakespeare Company presented it in 2012 to good reviews, while Shakespeare's Globe had a go in 2015 in time for the 800th anniversary of King John's reluctant signing of the Magna Carta. Both productions were well received, so perhaps there is life in the old king yet.

49. *HAMLET* IS THE MOST PERFORMED SHAKESPEARE PLAY EVER

If *King John* is our least favourite Shakespeare play, then *Hamlet* can certainly claim to be the one we love the most. The 1599 tale of a melancholy prince's revenge against his father's murderers begins on a cold, frosty night at Elsinore Castle in Denmark. Two night watchmen are feeling the chill when they encounter a ghost which turns out to be the restless spirit of Hamlet's father, the deceased king. Like all decent phantoms, he has an important message to pass on. It turns out that he was murdered by Hamlet's uncle Claudius. But that is not all. Not only has Claudius taken the king's life, he has also taken his throne and his wife Gertrude.

Hamlet decides to avenge his poor, murdered father. Several long soliloquies later, everyone ends up dead.

Hamlet was one of the most popular Shakespeare plays even in the playwright's own lifetime. The role was originally played by Richard Burbage, the foremost tragedian of the Chamberlain's Men, and enjoyed many outings on the Elizabethan and Jacobean stage. It was performed for James I in 1619. Since those early days the play has gained in popularity to the extent in which it is never off stage. Indeed, a production of *Hamlet* is said to be taking place somewhere around the world at any given time. 'To be, or not to be' are possibly the most famous lines in the English language.

Perhaps unsurprisingly, the most successful London productions over the last decade have normally included an A-list celebrity in the title role. In 2008 the actor David Tennant, at the time better known for his time-travelling antics as Doctor Who, starred in the Royal Shakespeare Company's modern-dress production of *Hamlet* in both Stratford and the West End. The show was credited with bringing a whole new audience to Shakespeare, with *Doctor Who* fans flocking to the show to see their hero Tennant in action. Reviewers at the time praised Tennant for bringing bittersweet humour and quicksilver wit to the role, his energy never waning for a moment. In a similar vein, productions starring Ben Whishaw, Christopher Eccleston and Samuel West have also dazzled the West End.

There is no doubt that *Hamlet* has caught the public imagination more than any other of Shakespeare's plays. What is it about Shakespearean tragedy that we love so much? According to an article written for the British Council by Professor Laura Eskill, Shakespeare's early audiences much preferred the history plays. She suggests this might be because issues of succession and royal power were so much more important in sixteenth-century England than they are today, which is a fair point. Whilst we in the modern world do not need to worry about the royal Windsors, who seem secure enough at Buckingham Palace, the themes in *Hamlet* are timeless. For as long as human beings tread the earth, someone, somewhere will be feeling the same emotions as Hamlet, even if only for a fleeting moment. That's cheery!

50. *HAMLET* WAS ALL ABOUT HAMNET

'Good Hamlet, cast thy knighted colour off, and let thine eye look like a friend on Denmark.' Hamlet's mother is telling him to stop moping. His father may have died recently, but life moves on doesn't it? Hamlet disagrees.

With its grief-stricken overtones, it is sometimes speculated that Shakespeare may have been thinking about a bereavement of his own whilst penning *Hamlet*. In 1585 Anne Hathaway gave birth to twins Judith and Hamnet, a girl and a boy. It is to be supposed that in this male-dominated age the couple would have been delighted with the birth of their first son. As cruel fate would have it, the boy Hamnet was also to be their last. He died just eleven years later of causes unknown. Child mortality rates were frighteningly high, with over 30 per cent of children never reaching adulthood, so his tragic demise would not have been entirely unexpected by the Shakespeare couple. Nevertheless, parental love does not change much throughout the ages; we can assume that Shakespeare took Hamnet's loss as a heavy blow.

So how might Shakespeare's grief have manifested itself? There is considerable speculation among scholars that he wrote the play *Hamlet* very much with the ghost of his dead son Hamnet in mind. It is a natural assumption. After all, the two names are very similar and were used interchangeably in Shakespeare's day. Also, the subject matter of the play, and Hamlet's agonised tussle with the facts surrounding his father's death, suggest a writer struggling with his own loss.

Compelling though the evidence may be, however, it is purely circumstantial and we should be careful not to assume too much about Shakespeare's life from his writing alone.

Instead, let's take a look at the historical background to *Hamlet*. The character of Hamlet was not a new invention. In fact, he dates back to the days of Scandinavian saga when the twelfth-century Danish writer Saxo Grammaticus wrote the tale of Amleth, a wronged prince whose father has been murdered and who descends into madness. Saxo's *Deeds of the Danes*, in which the tale first appeared, was printed in England in the sixteenth century as part of a collection of stories compiled by the French writer Francois de Belleforest. From there it was dramatised by Thomas Kyd in his *Ur-Hamlet* before Shakespeare picked up the baton and gave us his version of the story. With this in mind, it no longer seems so likely that Shakespeare was writing about his dead son. That is not to deny that he was ever inspired by his children – who can say what was going through his mind as he wrote? As well as the speculation about *Hamlet*, it is also suggested that Shakespeare had his twins in mind when he was writing *Twelfth Night*, a play in which Viola believes her twin brother has been drowned in a shipwreck. In the absence of any diaries or letters, searching for clues in the plays is irresistible.

51. Shakespeare Paid Tribute to His Murdered Colleague in *As You Like It*

Sometimes Shakespeare's 'clue dropping' was explicit enough to remove any doubt about who he was referring to. There is an intriguing passage in the play *As You Like It* which appears to point at a figure with whom Shakespeare was almost certainly acquainted. Here are the lines in question:

> When a man's verses cannot be understood, nor a man's good wit seconded with the forward child understanding, it strikes a man more dead than a great reckoning in a little room. Truly, I would the gods had made thee poetical.
> Touchstone, *As You Like It*, Act III, Scene III

On the face of it, these are some simple lines in which Touchstone complains about the country bumpkin Audrey's lack of understanding of his jokes. However, he uses interesting language, thick with playhouse references. He speaks of 'verses' and wishes that Audrey was had a more 'poetical' nature. Shakespeare almost certainly had his own versifying profession in mind when he wrote this. Things get interesting with his claim that lack of understanding 'strikes a man more dead than a great reckoning in a little room.' It is this line which makes scholars believe that Shakespeare had a specific playwright in mind; one who had recently suffered a violent death in controversial circumstances: Christopher Marlowe.

To understand what Shakespeare was talking about, we must go back to the year 1593. Christopher Marlowe was a widely recognised as a genius. Through groundbreaking classics such as *Tamburlaine* and *Doctor Faustus*, he helped pioneer the blank verse style so beloved of Shakespeare. If only he had limited his activities to the playhouse, things might have ended differently for Marlowe, but his restless curiosity saw him become embroiled in the dangerous world of state spying. The circumstances around his murder in 1593 are shrouded in mystery, but we know that on 30 May he travelled to a riverside house in Deptford where he spent all day drinking with three shady characters called Robert Poley, Nicholas Skeres, and Ingram Frizer. At some point a struggle ensued and Frizer stabbed Marlowe in the eye. According to the coroner's report the men had argued over the 'reckoning', or bill. While it is true that fights have occurred over smaller things, the underworld backgrounds of the men involved suggest there may have been more to it. Scholars still argue over what really happened.

What does seem clear, however, is that Marlowe was very much in his thoughts as Shakespeare wrote those lines in *As You Like It*. With his fondness for wordplay, the 'great reckoning in a little room' could refer either to the disputed bill, or perhaps a comeuppance. Neither is it the only reference to Marlowe in *As You Like It*. Shakespeare pays tribute to him with these lines which echo his poem Hero and Leander: 'Dead shepherd, now I find my saw of might, whoever loved that loved not at first sight?' There can be no doubt who the 'dead shepherd' is.

52. *RICHARD II* HELPED EXECUTE THE EARL OF ESSEX

'Oh lord, what fools these mortals be.' These words are spoken by the trickster Puck to his fairy king in *A Midsummer Night's Dream*. Puck was, of course, speaking about the sheer foolishness of human beings. Nowhere is this foolishness more evident than in those who chose to swim the waters of Tudor politics.

One such foolhardy adventurer who chose to enter into the 'Tempest' was Robert Devereaux, 2nd Earl of Essex. Robert was in many ways the very image of what we imagine a Tudor gentleman to be: tall, handsome, chivalrous and able to use his talents to good effect in the capture of Cadiz from the Spanish. This victory in the ongoing Anglo-Spanish wars saw him elevated to the status of national hero.

Of course, anyone who wanted to hold real power in late sixteenth-century England had to do business with the Virgin Queen, Elizabeth I. Like so many of her male courtiers, Robert was able to charm the queen. Sadly for Robert, however, his confidence was to be his undoing. He could be fiercely jealous, easily offended. His arrogance brought him into conflict with many, including the queen herself. On one occasion the earl offended her so much that she struck him round the face.

After a badly fought campaign in Ireland, Robert lost favour with the queen forever and she placed him under house arrest. It was during this spell that he plotted to use the playhouse as a secret weapon against the government. As a fan of the theatre, Robert recognised its power to win hearts and minds. He approached Shakespeare's company to perform the history play *Richard II*. The plot of the play involved the overthrow of a weak king who refused to listen to advice. Indeed the plot was to prove a very dangerous subject, so much so that the deposition scene in which Richard gives up his crown was normally cut from performances. The actors at first showed little interest in reviving the play, but Robert paid them forty shillings on top of the ticket sales for them to humour him – and to retain the deposition scene.

So the stage was set. The performance took place at the Globe on 7 February 1601. Sadly for Robert it was not money well spent. While it is true that Shakespeare could win hearts and minds, on this occasion the earl could not. When he and his merry band of 300 men marched on London the next day they found no support among the population. The rebels were greeted with sullen faces and closed doors. As Robert grew increasingly desperate his few supporters melted away. It was obvious whose side fortune favoured – and it was not the earl's. Quickly arrested, Robert was charged with treason. He was executed at Tower Hill on 25 February. This was a Shakespearean tragedy if ever there was one.

53. The First Performance of *The Comedy of Errors* Was a Riot

There is something delicious about the fact that the first known performance of *The Comedy of Errors* managed to live up to its name so spectacularly. It was a comedy of errors, indeed.

It happened on one raucous evening in the midst of the Christmas revels at Gray's Inn, one of London's four Inns of Court. As a proving ground for student lawyers, Gray's Inn were stuffed full of rich young men, hungry for fun. Traditionally students would remain on-site at mealtimes, gathering together in the great hall to dine at the long table. They made their own entertainment, producing student shows and plays. On the night of 28 December 1594, they were joined by Shakespeare's company, the Chamberlain's Men. It was the Feast of the Holy Innocents, an important date in the Christmas calendar and it seems the boys were in the mood for fun.

The chronicles of Gray's Inn, a document called 'Gesta Grayorum' note that the evening turned out to be a bit of a riot. The entry for that night says that 'a company of base and common players' came to perform and described how the evening began on a chaotic note with the audience of students invading the stage and breaking things. After this tumultuous prelude, 'a Comedy of Errors (much like Plautus his Menechmus) was played by the players. So that night was begun, and continued to the end, in nothing but confusion and errors, whereupon, it was ever afterwards called, The Night of Errors.'

There would have been sore heads in the morning.

54. He Was a Groom of the Chamber to James I

Queen Elizabeth I died in 1603 and was succeeded by James VI of Scotland, who rode down from Edinburgh with his wife Anne of Denmark and a train of followers. Keen to make a good impression on the English, he bestowed his royal favour liberally along the way, pardoning criminals and creating new knights. James was eager to reach London, describing his fortune as akin to 'swapping a stony couch for a deep feather bed'. Nevertheless he held his enthusiasm in check, waiting until the old queen had been buried before he made his grand entrance into the capital. It was a tactful move – Elizabeth had been a much-loved figurehead in England for over forty years. Perhaps with this in mind, James continued in the spirit of generosity, lavishing favours on his new English subjects. One of the beneficiaries was William Shakespeare and his company who found themselves translated to the King's Men; in other words they were now the king's personal troupe of players, effectively servants.

The royal patent was drawn up on 19 May naming Lawrence Fletcher, William Shakespeare, Richard Burbage, Augustine Philips, John Heminges, Henry Condell, William Sly, Robert Armin and Richard Cowley as Grooms of the Chamber. This was a symbolic position but meant the players were entitled to wear royal livery. They were duly sent along to the King's Wardrobe in Blackfriars to be fitted out with four and a half yards each of scarlet cloth.

King James's coronation was held on 25 July, and the King's Men played a key role in the pageantry of the day. It was traditional for monarchs to process through the streets of the City of London to show themselves to their new subjects before being crowned at Westminster. The streets were decked with banners and tapestries with seven triumphal arches lining the route. At several of these arches, actors from the King's Men performed symbolic pageants as James passed through. It was the beginning of the most illustrious era in Shakespeare's career. He was now officially a member of the royal household and some of his best writing was head of him.

James took full advantage of his new troupe of players, summoning them to perform at court with regularity. One of the most celebrated occasions was the Christmas holiday of 1603/1604 when the King's Men performed at Hampton Court Palace. There was plague in London so James had fled to the safety of his country retreat, bringing the whole court along with him. A letter from the courtier Dudley Carleton to his friend John Chamberlain says, 'On New Year's night we had a play of Robin Goodfellow.' This can only have been that Elizabethan classic, A Midsummer Night's Dream. The company performed in the magnificent hammer-beamed Great Hall, with its bright tapestries gleaming in the candlelight. It would have been a magical occasion, not just for the noble audience, but also for the newly elevated Shakespeare.

55. SHAKESPEARE TOOK *AS YOU LIKE IT* TO WILTSHIRE

We have the man Shakespeare with us ...

How tempting it is to envy the woman who is said to have written those words! Mary Sidney Herbert, the Countess of Pembroke, was an Elizabethan noblewoman who was renowned for her patronage of the arts. At her Wiltshire estate, Wilton House, she hosted a literary salon with a glittering guest list of names such as Edmund Spenser, Ben Jonson and Thomas Nashe. Poetry was in her genes: before his death at the Battle of Zutphen her brother Sir Philip Sidney had been celebrated for his prose romance *Arcadia*, written while staying with his sister at Wilton in 1580. Mary herself was the author of works such as *The Doleful Lay of Clorinda*. It would therefore seem entirely natural for her to have 'the man Shakespeare' at her house.

In the autumn of 1603 the London playhouses had been forcibly closed after an outbreak of the plague. It was a sensible measure; gathering together thousands of people in an enclosed space would allow the contagion to spread. The lack of venues in which to perform was clearly an inconvenience but it also presented an opportunity for the King's Men to tour – and to escape the plague. That autumn Shakespeare and his colleagues left London and did just that. They stopped at Mortlake in Surrey then moved onto Wilton House where they performed for King James on 2 December. A nineteenth-century historian, William Cory, added some colour to this account. He had spent time as a tutor at Wilton House and claimed to have seen a letter written by Mary Sidney to her son, bidding him to invite King James and Queen Anne to her house to see a performance of *As You Like It*. This is when she is supposed to have dangled the playwright as bait: 'We have the man Shakespeare with us.'

Unfortunately the letter is lost, if it ever existed, but the scenario seems plausible enough. If true, then Shakespeare's name and reputation must have been known well enough by his contemporaries for him to be an enticing draw. It is easy to imagine the King's Men performing the pastoral comedy *As You Like It* in such a bucolic setting. The hunting-mad King James would have appreciated the references in the play to his favourite sport:

Come, shall we kill us a venison?
And yet it irks me the poor dappled fools,
Being native burghers of this desert city,
Should in their own confines with forked heads
Have their round haunches gorged.
Duke Senior, *As You Like It,* Act II, Scene I.

Presumably the King's Men performed in the Great Hall, a room that is now sadly missing at Wilton House, a victim of seventeen century demolition and rebuilding. The hall was replaced with what is now a light and airy front hall. In the centre is a statue of Mary Sidney Herbert's most famous visitor, William Shakespeare. It is as if he had never left.

56. THE REIGN OF JAMES I WAS A REAL TRAGEDY

Things were not all sweetness and light, however; the reign of James I heralded some of Shakespeare's darkest writing. Looking at Shakespeare's pattern of writing from a distance of 400 years, we can see an interesting evolution in his work. While the Elizabethan years enjoyed an outpouring of comedies and histories, the Jacobean years were preoccupied with tragedy. From 1604 until his death in 1616, Shakespeare wrote plays such *King Lear, Macbeth, Measure for Measure, Othello,* and *The Tempest*; all of which deal with such dark themes as discord, injustice and jealousy.

Shakespeare was not the only one turning his hand to more serious subject matter. The reign of James I saw writers begin churning out so called 'Revenge Tragedies', a relatively new genre characterised by feuds, vengeance and grisly murder. Dating back to the Roman period and Seneca, the first Revenge Tragedy to grace the Early Modern stage was *The Spanish Tragedy* by Thomas Kyd. Shakespeare's own *Hamlet* and *Titus Andronicus,* with its multiple deaths and unstoppable cycle of retribution, also fit neatly into the Revenge Tragedy genre. It was not until the Jacobean years, however, that this bloodthirsty type of play really caught the public imagination. The reason this became a trend in James's reign may be partially explained by the king's own obsession with the dark side; he loved learning about witchcraft. On top of this, his initial popularity had begun to wane. The favouritism James showed to his Scottish followers led to a general feeling that his court was filled with corruption.

Here are a few examples of popular Revenge Tragedies in James's reign:

The Revenger's Tragedy: For a Revenge Tragedy, Thomas Middleton's play was very aptly named indeed. First performed in 1606, it is a dark tale of poisoning, rape, suicide and lust at an Italian court. The plot is a tangled web of revenge and counter revenge culminating in the murder of most of the main characters while the heroes Vindice and Hippolitio find themselves executed. There are no happy endings in revenge tragedy!

The Duchess of Malfi: John Webster's tragedy was written in 1612 and makes for a fairly disturbing read. The Duchess is under pressure from her brothers to remain unmarried but she defies them and marries her steward Antonio. When the marriage is discovered – as it was bound to be, especially after she becomes pregnant – her unhinged brother Ferdinand confronts her. Fearing for her life, the Duchess flees but is caught and imprisoned before being strangled to death.

'Tis Pity She's a Whore: Similarly grim is this 1629 play by John Ford. *'Tis Pity She's a Whore* begins with Giovanni confessing that he is in love with his sister Annabella. The two siblings begin an incestuous relationship while Annabella's various suitors go on a killing spree. Giovanni stabs Annabella to death and skewers her heart. A massacre ensues.

The outlandish plots and grisly endings of Revenge Tragedies make Shakespeare's most blood-spattered works seem quite tame in comparison.

57. He Was One of the First Englishmen to Promote the Idea of a United Kingdom

The 'Revenge Tragedy' was not King James's only contribution to the culture of the country. He effected a much more profound change simply by uniting the two crowns of England and Scotland. For an island raised on the idea that the two nations were separate, foreign entities, this was dramatic enough, but James's ambitions for Britain went much further. England and Scotland may have shared a monarch but they were functioning as individuals, each with their own separate parliaments and coins.

James saw no sense in this. In his effort to reinforce a feeling of national unity and togetherness he introduced a new coin called the 'Unite', and invoked the spirit of his ancestor Henry VII who 'reunited and confirmed in me the union of the two houses of Lancaster and York, whereof that king, of happy memory, was the first uniter'. Warming to his theme of unity, James went on to assert that 'the union of these two princely houses is nothing comparable to the union of two ancient and famous kingdoms'. The benefits of a united kingdom were clear to James. Essentially there was strength in numbers; it was far wiser to have one large country working together as one than remain fragmented. He also pointed out our similarities: 'Hath not God first united these two kingdoms both in language, religion and similitude of manners? Yea, hath he not made us all in one island, compassed in one sea.'

It was a charm offensive, a heartfelt campaign for unity. James's servant Shakespeare appears to have picked up on it. In 1605 he began writing the tragedy

King Lear. As all good Shakespeare fans will know, the plot revolves around Lear's unwise division of his kingdom. The old king has decided it is time to retire and calls in his three daughters, Goneril, Cordelia and Regan, for a meeting. He intends to divvy up the kingdom between them; this way he can leave all the cares of state behind whilst enriching his daughters. It is a generous offer. Vain as Lear is, however, he demands that his daughters shower him in praise before receiving their share. Goneril and Regan play their part well but Cordelia refuses to indulge in flattery and is banished without a penny. Lear's retirement plans go awry when Goneril and Regan turn against him and begin to make his life a misery. He flees with only his fool and the nobleman Kent for company. Meanwhile, Cordelia returns to England at the head of an army, intent on rescuing her father from this ignoble turn of events. In the best tradition of Shakespearean tragedy, they all end up dead with the exception of Kent, Edgar and Albany.

So, this is what happens when you divide a kingdom – it all ends in tears. In writing *King Lear* at such a sensitive moment in history, Shakespeare was adding his voice to an unstoppable movement. The Act of Union in 1707 finally sealed the deal, uniting the two kingdoms (for the time being, at least).

58. When Writing *King Lear*, Shakespeare Was Inspired by a Man Called Bryan

The setting of *King Lear* is pre-Roman Britain, an era shrouded in the mists of time. Shakespeare's tale was not new; like most of his plots, he adapted it from stories that had already been written, specifically the Elizabethan play *King Leir* which is thought to date from 1594. Leir and Lear tell the same story but with a crucial difference. While 'Leir' has a happy ending – Cordelia survives and Leir regains his throne – Shakespeare's version of the story is bleak and hopeless, as we saw in the previous chapter.

We do not know who wrote *King Leir* but what we do know is that the author was inspired by an imaginative medieval monk. Geoffrey of Monmouth was an eleventh-century Benedictine brother whose chronicle *Historia Regum Britanniae* told the story of the kings of Britain, both mythical and historical, from the Trojans to the early Anglo-Saxons. In 1135, when he created the work, his readers took the stories as fact, and thus figures such as King Arthur gained a foothold in the public imagination. King Lear was another of these mythical heroes.

So it was Geoffrey of Monmouth who gave us the rough outline of Lear's story, but perhaps Shakespeare's true inspiration was less Geoffrey of Monmouth than Bryan Annesley from Kent.

The strange story began in 1603. Sir Bryan Annesley of Kent was an elderly gentleman, honourably retired from the court of Elizabeth I. As the queen's Master of the Harriers he had led an active life but was now suffering the onset of senility. He had made his will, leaving the bulk of his possessions to his youngest daughter Cordelia. Can you see where this is going? That's right, he had two other daughters as well, and they were not amused at being left out. Perhaps Sir Bryan assumed they would manage; after all, they had both married well. Cordelia on the other hand was still single and would presumably suffer more in the event of her father's death.

That unhappy day came in 1604, and Sir Bryan's daughter Grace immediately contested the will, claiming that he was too senile to have known what he was doing. Even worse, when she went to the house to take an inventory of his goods, her youngest sister obstructed her. Grace described what happened in a letter to Robert Cecil, railing against the apparent injustice of it. Her frustration is evident, the tone evoking the usual complaints of those who take it upon themselves to dispute wills:

> We repaired unto the house of Bryan Annesley ... and finding him fallen into such imperfection & distemperature of mind and memory as we thought him thereby become altogether unfit to govern himself or his estate, we endeavoured to take a perfect inventory of such goods and chattels as he possessed ...

There was a happy ending to this. Cordelia responded with a letter of her own and successfully defended her legacy.

59. HE GOT THE IDEA FOR THE WITCHES IN *MACBETH* FROM THREE BOYS IN OXFORD

For people in Early Modern Britain, the phenomenon of witchcraft was a very real concern. Those accused were predominantly women, although men were not immune from the charge and, by looking at the trial records of the sixteenth and seventeenth centuries, we can see how frighteningly easy it was for someone to find themselves tied to a stake or dunked in a river. The causes of this 'witch craze' have been argued over for years now and nobody seems to have a definitive answer, but it is interesting to note the sheer number of accusations which arose in times of local difficulty. An unexplained harvest failure, the death of a cow, the sudden death of a newborn baby; none of these could have been God's work – it had to have been the devil. At this point, the local 'wise woman' or herbalist might find herself publicly denounced. It must have been terrifying for all concerned.

King James did not help matters. As a keen observer of witchcraft, he wrote a book on the subject in 1599 called *Daemonology* in which he advocated for the practice of witch hunting.

Shakespeare must have had his king's witch obsession in mind when he wrote *Macbeth*, as the play is totally steeped in the supernatural. The three witches, or weird sisters, cast their dark shadow over proceedings, prophesying first Macbeth's ascent to power, and then his downfall. They cast some scary sounding spells too: 'Round about the cauldron go; in the poisoned entrails throw.' This was perfect fodder for King James – especially given the relative brevity of the play. His attention span was short.

In Act I, Scene III, the witches meet Macbeth for the first time and deliver some happy news – he is going to become king. They hail him in turn:

> First Witch: All hail, Macbeth! Hail to thee, thane of Glamis!
> Second Witch: All hail, Macbeth! Hail to thee, thane of Cawdor!
> Third Witch: All hail Macbeth, that shall be king hereafter!

Shakespeare may have got the inspiration for the 'all hails' from a pageant which was laid on King James in 1605. The king and his wife, Anne of Denmark, spent that summer on a royal progress around the country, meeting their new subjects. On 27 August, they entered the city of Oxford where they heard a speech delivered by three boys outside St John's College. The actors delivered scripted lines to each other as dialogue before turning to the royal visitors and 'hailing' them in turn, predicting long life and happiness.

> His majesty passed along til he came before Saint John's College, when three little boys, coming forth of a castle made all of ivy, dressed like three nymphs (the conceit whereof the king did very much applaud), delivered three orations, first in Latin to the king, then in English to the queen and young prince; which being ended, his majesty proceeded towards the east gate of the city.

Shakespeare and his company passed through Oxford shortly afterwards where they would have heard the story. He wrote *Macbeth* the following year.

60. It is Unlucky to Say 'Macbeth'

Those of you familiar with the delightful BBC comedy *Blackadder* may remember a particular episode from Season Three. In this episode, Prince George hires two actors to try and improve his bad public image, much to the annoyance of his butler Blackadder. Our scheming hero quickly finds out that the two actors have a weakness: they freak out at the mention of one of Shakespeare's plays. The work in question is *Macbeth*.

The reason for their frightened reaction is that, according to theatre tradition, the name of Macbeth is said to be cursed. Anyone foolish enough to speak the name 'Macbeth' aloud risks bringing down bad luck on themselves and others. Many actors will only say 'Macbeth' during rehearsals or live performances. The rest of the time it is simply called 'The Scottish Play'.

The origins of this rather strange but interesting story go back to the very beginning when the great playwright first penned the play. Opening night was fast approaching when disaster struck. Legend says that the actor who was meant to play Lady Macbeth was struck down with fever and died. This of course caused Shakespeare to have to recast the part at the last minute. In the years that followed others who took the part in the play would meet with similar misfortune. One story from seventeenth-century Amsterdam saw the actor who played Duncan die live on stage. As many of you know, Duncan is murdered to make way for the treacherous Macbeth's assent to the throne and the choice of weapon employed was a dagger. Somehow during this performance of the play the prop knife had been switched with a real one. This was either a case of Method Acting going to the extreme or something more sinister. Neither are these misfortunes are not just relegated to the distant past. In 2013 a performance of *Macbeth* in Manchester starring Kenneth Branagh saw one of his co-stars taken to hospital after he was struck with a sword during a battle scene. Thankfully the actor fared better than the unfortunate seventeenth-century Duncan, and went on to fight another day.

Why, then, is *Macbeth* believed to be cursed? Well, we have to remember that one of the key themes in *Macbeth* is witchcraft, and it was believed by some that Shakespeare had managed to get his hand on real spells to be used in the lines involving the three witches, thus imbuing the play with dark powers. Actors have found ways to protect themselves from the curse. If you say the name 'Macbeth' you should exit the theatre, spin around three times and then either say a line from Shakespeare – usually this one from *Hamlet*: 'Angels and ministry of grace defend us' – or if that is not your thing you let loose a curse word. Maybe the curse is just a story. Or maybe, just maybe there are more things in heaven and earth than are dreamed of in our philosophy.

King James had barely been on the throne of England for two years before some of his subjects tried to blow him off it again. On the night of 5 November 1605, a strange man was found lurking in the shadows of a cellar beneath the House of Lords. He was cloaked and his spurs jangled upon his boots as if ready for sudden flight. The soldiers shone their lanterns around the room and quickly found the reason for his haste. There, hidden beneath piles of faggots, were thirty-six barrels of gunpowder. The man's fuse was ready to be lit.

He was swiftly arrested and taken to the Tower of London where he calmly confessed that his intention had been to blow up the Houses of Parliament, killing King James and all the assembled lords at the state opening. When asked his name, he replied, 'John Johnson.' Of course, we all know his real name. This was Guy Fawkes, a man whose name would soon be infamous.

The Gunpowder Plot was a reaction to King James's harsh laws against Catholics but it also had xenophobic undertones, with Fawkes stating that he wished to blow King James and his fellow Scots back to the mountains. Fawkes did not act alone, however. He was just the foot soldier in a plot which had been simmering since May 1604, when the ringleaders held their first meeting at the Duck and Drake on the Strand. They were quite fond of meeting in taverns. On 9 October 1605, just weeks before the intended blow, Shakespeare's friend Ben Jonson was seen dining with some of the conspirators at the Irish Boy. It is interesting that Jonson was not arrested after the plot's discovery. Instead the government drew on his help, sending him out to search for Catholic priests. It may be no coincidence that he was fresh out of prison for insulting King James with anti-Scottish jokes in the play *Eastward Ho*; perhaps spying had been a condition of his release. Whatever the reason, Jacobean England was a small world of interconnecting associations and friendships. It may be a slight exaggeration to say that he was friends with Guy Fawkes but Shakespeare certainly knew the ringleader, Robert Catesby. A Warwickshire man, Catesby was born in the village of Lapworth, not far from Stratford-upon-Avon. Back in 1581, when the Jesuit priest Edmund Campion had travelled through the Midlands distributing illicit Catholic literature, he had stayed with Catesby's father Sir William. Shakespeare's father John is believed to have been one of those who paid the priest a visit at Lapworth, taking away his copy of Cardinal Borromeo's *Testament*. As we saw earlier, this tract was later found hidden in the roof at Henley Street. Catesby was not the only conspirator associated with Shakespeare. John Grant was from Norbrook near Snitterfield – John Shakespeare's village – and was acquainted with the family through various business transactions. The Grants were also related by marriage to Shakespeare's kinsmen the Somervilles.

62. There Are Numerous Portraits of Shakespeare but We Still Don't Know What He Looked Like

One of the enduring frustrations for Shakespeare enthusiasts is that we have no idea what he actually looked like. Of all the portraits purported to show his likeness, not one has been officially accepted as Shakespeare. Things do get a little more promising if we are willing to move away from portraiture and into the realm of sculpture and engravings – the famous Droushout engraving which adorned the First Folio shows a balding man with bulbous eyes and a dome shaped head. It is rather two dimensional and not an especially satisfying image but Ben Jonson claimed it was a good likeness. The other supposedly accurate image is that of Shakespeare's memorial bust in Holy Trinity Church, Stratford. His widow Anne Hathaway is reported to have approved of it.

Neither the Droushout engraving nor the bust in Stratford gives us a good sense of what Shakespeare looked like in the flesh so let's turn to some of the portraits instead.

The Chandos Portrait: Everybody will know this portrait. It shows a thoughtful looking man with a domed forehead and receding hairline. Two bushy waves of black hair billow out on either side of his face and the collars of his white shirt are folded neatly over his sober black doublet. He has a clerkly air about him; this is someone with ink-stained fingers. What makes this image so compelling is the flash of brilliance suggested by the gold hooped earring he wears in his left ear. It is believed to have been painted sometime between 1600 and 1610 when Shakespeare was at the height of his success. It hangs in the National Portrait Gallery and the name 'Chandos' comes from its former owners.

The Cobbe Portrait: This one shows a much flashier gentleman. Named after its former owner Charles Cobbe, this portrait is thought to date back to 1610. It shows a neatly coiffured figure with a trim beard and rosy cheeks. He is richly dressed in a gold trimmed doublet and huge lace collars which fan out over his shoulders, concealing his neck. It was passed down to the Cobbe family via the descendents of Shakespeare's patron Henry Wriothesley, 3rd Earl of Southampton.

The Sanders Portrait: The Sanders Portrait shows a plain-looking man whose bushy, unkempt hair recalls that of the Chandos portrait. His silver laced doublet and silk collar suggest a much wealthier subject than the black clad fellow in the Chandos portrait and a small smile plays about his lips. A small label at the back, thought to date to the seventeenth century, names the sitter as Shakespeare and says that 'this likeness (was) taken 1603'. If this is indeed Shakespeare, then one theory proposed by Jenny Tiramani of the Globe is that Shakespeare had it painted to mark his company's success in being named the King's Men.

At the time of writing none of these portraits has been definitively proven to be Shakespeare but they certainly help us imagine him.

63. HE WAS THE VICTIM OF IDENTITY THEFT

In 1605 a new play was published by Nathaniel Butter, a London stationer, and sold at the sign of the Bull in St Paul's Churchyard. *The London Prodigal* was a 'City Comedy', a genre dealing with the humorous antics of the merchants and bourgeoisie of London. City Comedies had been around for a few years but at the dawn of the seventeenth century they had gained in popularity, with playwrights such as Thomas Middleton and John Marston churning them out alongside their Revenge Tragedies. These comedies tended to have a cynical and satirical edge, mercilessly mocking the vices and hypocrisy of the age.

The storyline of the *London Prodigal* is fairly typical of its genre. It tells the tale of a merchant's son Matthew Flowerdale, who lives a life of debauchery and sin. He gambles, drinks, sleeps around, and generally has more fun than anyone else. Unknown to Matthew, his father decides to spy on him to discover the extent of his bad behaviour. Shocked and appalled by what he sees he can only hope that his 'prodigal son' will mend his ways. Meanwhile, Matthew decides he needs a rich wife to help him pay for his lifestyle. He deceives Sir Lancelot Spurcock into giving him his daughter in marriage, but his debts catch up with him and he is arrested on his wedding day. After a few more dirty tricks involving robbery and the attempted pimping of his wife, he finally sees the light and decides to become a better person. The prodigal son has returned.

The title cover of the play calls it 'The London Prodigal, as it was plaide by the King's Majesties servaunts.' That would be Shakespeare's company, The King's Men. Even more interesting, it claimed that the play was written 'by William Shakespeare'. Unfortunately the play was not included in the First Folio so scholars dispute that Shakespeare was the author. On the face of things it looks like another case of greedy publishers cashing in on the Shakespeare name, but unlike the previous occasions, this time the Bard did not complain. Could the publisher Nathaniel Butter have been telling the truth after all? Some people clearly thought so. In 1664 Philip Chetwynde published a third edition of the complete works of Shakespeare. This Third Folio contained *The London Prodigal* along with several other works of disputed authorship. The intriguing list of plays Chetwynde attributed to Shakespeare included titles such as *The History of Thomas, Lord Cromwell, The Puritan Widow, The Tragedy of Locrine,* and *A Yorkshire Tragedy.* If Chetwynd is to be believed, Shakespeare was even keener on tragedy than we thought. Collectively, these plays are known as the 'Shakespeare Apocrypha' as they had been published in Shakespeare's lifetime under the mysterious initials 'W. S.' Even so, Shakespeare was not the only man in Jacobean London to have these initials, and scholars have put forward two other names as possible authors of these plays. Step forward, Wentworth and William Smith.

64. He Acted as Cupid in a Real-Life Case of Two Star-Cross'd Lovers

Not content with dramatising the romantic troubles of Romeo and Juliet, it seems that Shakespeare was a dab hand at bringing young lovers together in real life.

Sometime in 1604, Shakespeare packed his trunk and moved out of his Bankside lodgings. For some reason he had decided to leave the entertainment district and move back into the City of London on the north side of the River Thames. He chose a quiet neighbourhood in the north-west corner of the city close to the old Roman wall which encircled the Square Mile. Anyone who has visited the Museum of London will have noticed the roaring thoroughfare called London Wall which runs adjacent. The area was very different in Shakespeare's day; in 1604, London Wall was Silver Street, the traditional home of the city's silversmiths. Shakespeare moved in with a family of French Huguenot refugees called the Mountjoys. Appropriately enough considering the history of the street, Christopher Mountjoy, the master of the house, earned his living as a tiara maker. His wife Marie was fond of astrology. She was a frequent visitor to the occultist Simon Forman but did not always receive pleasant predictions from him. On one occasion he told her she was pregnant – had his diagnosis been correct, it would have been bad news as Marie sometimes had illicit flings. She was lucky; there would be no illegitimate baby. The Mountjoys had just one child, a daughter called Mary.

Also in the household on Silver Street was an apprentice called Stephen Bellott. It is thanks to Bellott that we know of Shakespeare's stint in the household.

Eight years later, Bellott, by now no longer an apprentice at Silver Street, filed a lawsuit against Christopher Mountjoy. It is a fascinating story. Christopher and Marie Mountjoy had noticed that the young Bellot had feelings for their daughter. They must have had difficulty persuading him to marry her, however, as they turned to their lodger for help. Perhaps they were aware of his 'sugared sonnets' about the importance of marriage and procreation. More likely, they simply felt that he was good with words and would stand a better chance of selling the matrimonial state to the reluctant youngsters. Whichever approach he took in the end, it worked. Stephen Bellot and Mary Mountjoy were married at the little church across the road. There just was one snag. Christopher Mountjoy was now refusing to pay the bride's dowry.

Stephen Bellott took his father-in-law to court in pursuit of the money. Witnesses were called, one of whom deposed that, according to the lodger Shakespeare, Mountjoy had promised £50 to Bellott. When Shakespeare himself was called, however, he gave vague reponses to the questions, claiming not to remember how much the dowry was worth or by which date it was due to be paid. The court referred this strange case to the French church who ordered Mountjoy to pay up. A stingy man to the last, he managed to avoid doing so.

65. The Character Emilia in *Othello* Is Based on His Mistress

In an earlier chapter we explored the possibility that Shakespeare had an affair with the brothel keeper Lucy Morgan. Another name often mentioned in the same breath as Shakespeare is that of Emilia Lanier. Like Lucy, Emilia was another denizen of Clerkenwell, but rather than work the brothels, she was in the rather more fortunate position of having a regular keeper. For a period until 1592 she was the mistress of Henry Carey, the first Lord Hunsden. When she became pregnant by him he pensioned her off and arranged her marriage to a court musician, Alfonso Lanier. Two years later, Lord Hunsden would lend his noble name to Shakespeare's Company when they became the Chamberlain's Men.

Emilia came from a musical background. Descended from Italian Jews, her forebears had played at court since the reign of Henry VIII. Some scholars think Shakespeare may be alluding to her musicality in Sonnet 128:

> How oft when thou, my music, music play'st,
> Upon that blessed wood whose motion sounds
> With thy sweet fingers when thou gently sway'st
> The wiry concord that my ear confounds

Could she have been the Dark Lady of the sonnets? With their mutual connections to men such as Hunsden and the Henry Wriothesley, 3rd Earl of Southampton, Shakespeare and Emilia would have had ample opportunity to cross paths. They also had poetry in common. In 1611, Emilia wrote a proto-feminist volume entitled *Salve Deus Rex Judaeorum* which she dedicated to various noble women including the queen, Anne of Denmark, and Ben Jonson's patron Lucy of Bedford. With titles including *Eve's Apologie in Defence of Women*, Emilia stands up for women's rights. Mutinously, she asks, 'why are poor women blam'd, or by more faulty men defam'd?'

Intriguingly, some scholars argue that Shakespeare had this sparky poet in mind when he wrote the play *Othello*. It is easy to see why. The tragic tale of violent jealousy culminating in Othello's murder of his wife, Desdemona, may not be the most romantic of plays, but it contains possibly the most feminist speech in the whole of Shakespeare. The words are spoken by a character called Emilia:

> But I do think it is their husband's faults
> If wives do fall: say that they slack their duties,
> And pour our treasures into foreign laps,
> Or else break out in peevish jealousies,
> Throwing restraint upon us, or say they strike us ...
> ... Let husbands know
> Their wives have sense like them: they see and smell
> And have their palates both for sweet and sour,
> As husbands have.
> Emilia, *Othello*, Act IV, Scene III

Other clues in the text point to Emilia Lanier's Italian background. She was born Emilia Bassano, the daughter of a Venetian. Of course, *Othello* is partially set in Venice, but the character of the Moor himself is based upon the Jesuit Girolamo Otello who lived in the town of Bassano not far from Venice. It could all be a strange coincidence – but it seems unlikely.

66. Shakespeare Was Not the Only Shakespeare Making His Living from London Theatre

It is sometimes forgotten that William was not the only Shakespeare living in London and earning his living at the playhouse. Edmund Shakespeare, the playwright's brother, is known to have lived for a short time in the capital but the details of his life are even sketchier than William's. We know that he had an illegitimate son, Edward, who was still a baby when he died in 1607. We also know that Edmund followed him to the grave months later at the age of twenty-seven. What we don't know is when he came to London or how he and his son died. Thanks to the practice of only recording the father's name on baptismal records, we don't even know who Edward's mother was.

Although Edmund and William Shakespeare came from the same family and both worked in the same profession in the same town, the contrast in their circumstances is intriguing. Whilst William was making a good living as a shareholder on Bankside and building up a property portfolio, Edmund scratched a living as a jobbing actor, probably staying in rented digs. Like other members of the persecuted theatrical profession, he lived outside the city walls. His parish of Giles-without-Cripplegate was handily close to Shoreditch and the northern playhouses. The 'Cripple Gate' itself formed one of the entrances, or exits, through the wall; the name has obscure origins, but one theory says it comes from the Anglo-Saxon word *cruple* meaning covered walkway or tunnel.

It is curious to think that Edmund Shakespeare chose to base himself in Cripplegate, close to Edward Alleyn and the Fortune playhouse, when his big brother William was enjoying huge success at the Globe, his Bankside hit factory. Perhaps he wanted to keep some distance, to assert his independence. Or maybe William was unwilling, or unable, to help. Some writers have suggested that they had a strained relationship. Why else would William have named the bitter, jealous, illegitimate brother in King Lear 'Edmund?'

There is a poignant post-script to that obscure young man's life, however. After his untimely death his big brother stepped in to take care of the funeral arrangements and, it has to be said, he made rather a good job of it. Just before noon on 31 December 1607 the great bell of St Saviour's (now Southwark Cathedral) rang out across Southwark, a call to all those who wished to pay their respects to come together. Funerals were normally held in the afternoon but in the case of someone like Edmund Shakespeare, whose mourners were drawn from the theatrical crowd, it made sense for it to take place before performances began at the local playhouses. Shakespeare had ensured that Edmund's funeral was announced in style, paying the lavish sum of twenty shillings for the great bell to be rung. Whatever differences may have existed between the two brothers, they were surely forgotten now. A memorial stone to Edmund can be seen in the choir of Southwark Cathedral.

67. Shakespeare Was a Solitary Writer

In fact, he was not at all solitary. The life was an Early Modern playwright was a collaborative effort requiring disparate groups of people – and their egos – to work closely together in a spirit of cooperation. Not only did he have to work with his fellow actors and shareholders at the Globe, but he also worked with other playwrights. Whether he was contributing scenes to their work or accepting contributions from them, Shakespeare was part of a network of writers all dipping their quills into each other's pots of ink.

Let's have a look at some of the plays which he created with a little help from his friends.

Henry VI: Part I: Written very early in Shakespeare's career, some scholars believe it is a patchwork of scenes written by other writers, including Thomas Nashe, and revised by Shakespeare.

Pericles, Prince of Tyre: Ben Jonson described *Pericles* as a 'mouldy tale', which may sound harsh, but it is true all the same. Rarely performed, it is a play of two halves. Shakespeare is generally believed to have written the second half while the author of the first half was a Clerkenwell brothel keeper called George Wilkins. Among his many criminal charges was that of kicking a pregnant woman in the stomach.

Macbeth: In recent years scholars have found compelling textual evidence to suggest that Thomas Middleton contributed some scenes to Shakespeare's Scottish play. The passage in which Hecate sings a magical song is believed to have been added at a later date. The first two lines of her song are very apt for a work of collaboration:

> O well done! I commend your pains;
> And everyone shall share i' the gains.

Henry VIII: John Fletcher was Shakespeare's partner on this tale of intrigue at the Tudor court. He is most famous for his enduring partnership with Francis Beaumont with whom he lodged at a house on Bankside.

The Two Noble Kinsmen: First performed by the King's Men at the Blackfriars playhouse, the 1634 title page of this play attributes it to 'the memorable worthies of their time, Mr John Fletcher and Mr William Shakespeare'.

The Spanish Tragedy: Thomas Kyd's Elizabethan revenge tragedy was so popular it was constantly revived on stage. In 1602 the publisher Thomas Pavier reprinted it with five additional passages thought to have been penned by Shakespeare.

Timon of Athens: As well as helping out with *Macbeth*, Thomas Middleton is also thought to have contributed his genius to the sad tale of Timon. It is a patchy play with a strange, unsatisfactory ending leading scholars to believe that two heads were involved rather than just one. Middleton has been identified as the other contributor thanks to close analysis of the text which has highlighted similarities to his style.

So, it seems that Shakespeare was far from a solitary writer. He was a hack – a collaborator like everyone else. The image of Shakespeare as a precious diva, agonising alone in his garret, could not be further from the truth.

68. The Plays *All's Well that Ends Well*, *Measure for Measure*, and *The Winter's Tale* Are Real Problems

We twenty-first-century humans are a funny lot. Like frustrated librarians, we like to put everything from people to plays into neat little boxes. It helps us make sense of things. Some things, however, defy order and constraint. Take the works of Shakespeare, for example. We generally place his plays into three distinct categories: Tragedy, Comedy, and History. An unfortunate result of this fastidiousness is that his dense and complex worlds find themselves hemmed in by our expectations of the genre.

When things don't quite fit, we call it a 'Problem Play.' Examples of Shakespeare's 'Problem Plays' include *Measure for Measure*, *All's Well that Ends Well*, and *Troilus and Cressida*, all of which contain enough light and shade to confuse the critics. Are these tragedies or comedies? Nobody can quite decide. Let's take *Measure for Measure*, a play filled with dark humour and disturbing themes. Claudio is arrested and sentenced to death for the crime of fornication. His sister Isabella, a novice nun, pleads with the governor Angelo to spare him. He refuses, saying that Claudio needs to be made an example of. At this point Angelo decides to test his power over the distraught Isabella. He tells her that if she yields her virginity to him, her brother might be saved. Imagine doing that to a nun! Shakespeare is shining a light on the hypocrisy of the age. The play is believed to date to around 1604, a period in which King James was enacting similarly harsh laws against fornication and brothel-keeping. A comic sub-plot involving the bawd Mistress Overdone and her pals Pompey and Elbow brings light relief to the action, but the humour is still tinged with cynicism.

Then we have *All's Well that Ends Well* with its forced marriage. The jokes come thick and fast but who can fail to feel indignant on behalf of Bertram who is pressured into marrying Helena, a woman he does not love? He goes unwillingly to the altar before fleeing off to war. Helena follows him and tricks him into consummating the marriage. Poor, defeated Bertram agrees to try and be a worthy husband. *All's Well* was classified as a comedy in the First Folio but, unlike the joyous *A Midsummer Night's Dream,* or *The Comedy of Errors,* the ending to this play leaves rather a bad taste in the mouth.

Another play sometimes described as a 'problem' is *The Winter's Tale*, a drama whose mood suddenly switches from tense and moody in the first three acts to light and pastoral in the final two. Like *All's Well That Ends Well, The Winter's Tale* was listed as a comedy in the First Folio but is usually categorised as a Romance along with Shakespeare's other later plays such as *Cymbeline* and *The Tempest.*

The term 'Problem Play' was first coined in 1896 by Frederick Boas, but the playwright himself saw things in a more fluid light. A piece of work could easily be described as tragical-comical, historical-tragical, or even comical-historical.

69. SHAKESPEARE'S WISEST CHARACTERS WERE FOOLS

A fool thinks himself to be wise, but a wise man knows himself to be a fool. This was a line spoken by Touchstone, a character in William Shakespeare's play *As You Like It*, and in many ways it sums up his fools to a tee. Shakespeare was a great lover of themes in his plays and the character of the 'wise fool' was no exception.

As court jester to Duke Frederick, Touchstone is one of Shakespeare's best-loved fools; but he was no stereotypical buffoon. Unlike other Shakespearean fools, he did not engage in pranks and practical jokes. His humour came instead from his natural wit and insight into human nature, often seeing the irony in situations when his noble companions did not. Touchstone's use of puns highlights the Elizabethan love of wordplay. Indeed, he loves to twist words to the point of driving others to near madness. Even the name 'Touchstone' holds deeper meaning – a touchstone was used to determine the purity of metals, just as the fool in the play was used to determine the purity and truth of the other characters.

Another jester who was to play a pivotal role in Shakespeare's work was the trickster fairy Puck, who embodies two themes which Shakespeare seemed to love to employ in his work, the supernatural and the fool. Puck is the jester and right-hand man to Oberon, King of the Fairies and is in many ways the key character of *A Midsummer Night's Dream*. His games and mischief unleash much of the humour and chaos upon the other protagonists of the story, for example turning Bottom's head into that of a donkey and mistakenly administering the love juice to Lysander instead of Demetrius, causing him to fall in love with Helena. While more mischievous than nasty, Puck's character is a contradiction in that he is both good natured but still capable of spiteful pranks. He revels in the madness he has unleashed and only sets things right by the order of his king.

It is widely believed that the role of the wise fool in Shakespeare owes much to a man by the name of Robert Armin. Originally an apprentice goldsmith, many believe the role of Touchstone was created specifically with Armin in mind. Shakespeare saw the comic master for what he was and shaped the role to suit Armin's style of acting, incorporating his wit, intelligence and charm. Indeed, Armin went on to play the wise fool in other Shakespeare plays such the Fool in *King Lear*. Such is the Fool's wisdom, he is the only one who can get away with expressing any form of criticism of proud old Lear. He is loyal, too, staying by his master's side through thick and thin. In Shakespeare land, a fool is the best sort of friend to have. Wise, irreverent, and unafraid to tell it like is, they embody the spirit of Shakespeare in a nutshell.

70. DESPITE SETTING MOST OF HIS PLAYS IN FOREIGN COUNTRIES HIS GEOGRAPHY WAS TERRIBLE (HIS HISTORY WAS TOO)

It is fair to say that Shakespeare's fellow playwright Ben Jonson was a stickler for geographical accuracy. Three years after Shakespeare's death, Jonson walked to Scotland to visit his friend William Drummond. It was the Christmas season and he was in the mood for a good old gossip, undoubtedly with a tumbler or two of whisky to hand. Drummond recorded their conversations, some of which were fairly scurrilous in nature. For example, Jonson claimed that Elizabeth I had been physically incapable of taking a husband 'for she had a membrana on her which made her incapable of men'.

The late queen was not the only subject of his gossip. He went on to mock his old friend Shakespeare's geographical mistakes: 'Shakespeare in a play brought in a number of men saying they had suffered shipwreck in Bohemia, where there is no sea nearby some 100 miles.'

Jonson was referring *The Winter's Tale*, a play set in an alternative version of Bohemia, one which Shakespeare describes as a 'desert country near the sea'. Now as we all know, Bohemia is landlocked, but it is easy enough to suspend disbelief with Shakespeare. Geographical correctness should be the least of our worries; after all, this is a world in which a statue of Hermione comes to life. Nevertheless, it was the coastline and the shipwreck which bothered Ben Jonson. In Act III, Scene III, the Clown is describing the scene:

I would you did but see how it chafes, how it rages, how it takes up the shore! But that's not the point. O,

the most piteous cry of the poor souls! Sometimes to
see 'em, and not to see 'em; now the ship boring the
moon with her main-mast and anon swallowed with
yest and froth.

Perhaps Jonson was right to mock. If Shakespeare's
Bohemian geography was bad, then his knowledge of
Italy's geography was even worse. A good proportion
of Shakespeare's plays are set at least partially in
Italy but our hero still makes the odd gaff. In *The
Tempest*, for example, Prospero sets sail from Milan
to the Adriatic Sea, although it has been argued that
Shakespeare may have had the inland canal system in
mind. Another example is seen in *The Two Gentlemen
of Verona* when Valentine sails to Verona from Milan.

When it came to writing history plays, Shakespeare
was on firmer ground, consulting *Holinshead's
Chronicles* for a reasonably accurate narrative of events.
In *Richard III*, however, Prince Edward is wrongly told
that Julius Caesar built the Tower of London. We
know that it was built by William the Conqueror. One
of the Roman plays contains an infamous howler. In
Act II, Scene V of *Antony and Cleopatra*, the Egyptian
queen calls her woman Charmian away for a game of
billiards, something which was only invented in the
fifteenth century.

In conclusion, Shakespeare may have veered into
fantasy on occasion but he is all the more charming for
it. Now, who's for billiards?

71. He Had an Illegitimate Son Called William Who Also Became a Playwright

Samuel Pepys had a good day on 24 August 1661. In the morning he went to Captain Holmes's house to see a strange creature called a baboon, then in the evening he headed off to the theatre to watch *Hamlet*. The star actor was Thomas Betterton and the producer was William Davenant. Pepys enjoyed the show, pronouncing it was 'done with scenes very well'. Two years later the same team put on an adaptation of *Macbeth*. It was strange choice; Shakespeare had been dead for half a century and Restoration audiences thought he was a bit old hat. It seems that Davenant, however, had personal reasons for keeping his memory alive.

The story begins on Bankside in the late sixteenth century. Davenant's parents, John and Jane, were merchant vinters living in the heart of later Elizabethan theatre land. It is likely they would have known Shakespeare as he also lived in the area. In 1600 the couple moved to Oxford to take up a tenancy at the Crown Tavern. Part of New College, it was a large, comfortable inn with twenty rooms and conveniently placed as a stopover for travellers journeying between London and the Midlands. It appears to have suited Shakespeare perfectly. The seventeenth century gossip John Aubrey stated that, 'Mr William Shakespeare was wont to go into Warwickshire once a year and did commonly in his journey lie in this house in Oxon where he was exceedingly respected. I have heard Parson Robert say that Mr William Shakespeare has given (Davenant) a hundred kisses.' It is easy to imagine the weary traveller greeting an enthusiastic child with kisses on his annual journey through town but Davenant appeared to think there was more to it than simple friendliness. In a letter to a friend he said, 'know this which does honour to my mother – I am the son of Shakespeare.' Was he speaking figuratively? Perhaps he was. According to the poet Samuel Butler, 'it seemed to Davenant that he writ with the same spirit Shakespeare did.' Nevertheless, if there were any rumours that Davenant was Shakespeare's illegitimate child, he did nothing to discourage them.

Davenant had been born in 1606, and after his parents' death moved to London where he began to forge his successful theatre career. He found favour at court and by 1638 had succeeded Ben Jonson in the role of Poet Laureate. Like all those in the theatrical industry his livelihood took a blow when Oliver Cromwell closed the playhouses but matters improved with the restoration of the monarchy. Under licence from Charles II he shared a duopoly of the theatre with Thomas Killigrew.

As for his true paternity, that remains a mystery. It is a romantic idea to imagine William Shakespeare fathering a fellow playwright but the fact remains that Shakespeare himself did not claim Davenant as a son, and so the mystery lingers on.

72. He Helped to Write the Bible

Shakespeare may not have written the Ten Commandments – nor been much good at keeping them, if we are to believe William Davenant's tale of adultery in Oxfordshire – but some say that he had a hand in writing one of the English translations of the Bible. Those who support the idea that he contributed to the King James Bible point to Psalm 46 which contains the name 'Shakespeare' albeit in two separate parts and on two different lines. Have a look at these lines:

God is our refuge and strength, a very present help in trouble,
Therefore will we not fear, though the earth be
removed, and though the mountains
Be carried into the midst of the sea;
Though the waters thereof roar and be troubled,
Though the mountains SHAKE ...
... He maketh wars to cease unto the end of the earth,
He breaketh the bow, and cutteth the SPEAR in
sunder.

The capitals are mine and, as you can see, highlight the name of a certain playwright. The forty-sixth word from the beginning of the psalm is 'shake' and, if you count back from the end, the forty-sixth word is 'spear' if you ignore the obscure liturgical punctuation word 'selah'. In 1611, when the King James Bible was completed, Shakespeare just so happened to be forty-six years old. Is this just coincidence, or is it proof that Shakespeare was even more multi-talented than we had ever imagined? It is easy to understand why some people believe that Shakespeare wrote the psalm. The King James Bible is rightly cherished for its contribution to the English language and the beauty of some of the phrasing. It would seem natural for our greatest poet to have been involved. Sadly, it seems like little more than wishful thinking.

Back in 1604 when James I hosted the conference at Hampton Court Palace he had spent time listening to some of the concerns of the Puritan faction in the Church of England. They did not approve of some of the wording in the existing Bible translations and wanted a brand new version. Eager to keep everyone happy, James commissioned forty-seven clerical scholars to set about writing it. The task was huge. Not only did the scholars have to translate the Old and New Testaments from the original Greek and Aramaic, they also had to work together to agree upon changes and to check each other's work. The job was not made any easier by the fact that they were split up into six committees in three different English cities: Oxford, Cambridge, and London.

The final version was approved by yet another committee who met at the Stationer's Hall in Blackfriars. The King James Bible introduced new words and phrases into English such as 'salt of the earth' and 'give up the ghost.' It was a magnificent achievement but Shakespeare had nothing to do with it. We know exactly who the translators were and none of them went by the name of Shakespeare.

73. *Hamlet* Was Performed in 1607 – in a Ship off the Coast of Africa

Shakespeare was used to touring around the country, bringing his genius to far-flung counties across the whole of England. He must have felt like a rock star – if it's Oxford today, it must be Banbury tomorrow; phew! This was glamorous enough but he may not have realised exactly far his name had spread.

In the late summer of 1607 the crew of two ships on their way to the East Indies became stricken with scurvy. In order to boost the men's vitamin intake, William Keeling, the expedition commander ordered both vessels, the *Red Dragon* and the *Hector*, to drop anchor in a Sierra Leone estuary where they would have access to a plentiful supply of citrus fruits. Whilst they were cooling their heels off the coast of Africa, the crew decided to have some entertainment with feasting and plays. Keeling extended an invitation to the locals and four royal delegates boarded the *Red Dragon*. They were sent over to the *Hector* for some food before boarding the *Red Dragon* again to watch the crew perform in a play. This play was the 'tragedie of Hamlett'. The following month they performed another Shakespeare classic, *Richard II*. Keeling appears to have had an ulterior motive in encouraging his crew to learn Shakespeare, stating that it kept 'my people from idleness and unlawful games, or sleep'. The next time someone complains that Shakespeare sends them to sleep, it might be useful to remind them of this.

It would be interesting to know how *Hamlet* was received by the four Sierra Leoneans. As a European colony, their language was Portuguese so they may have had difficulty with some of *Hamlet*'s longer soliloquies. We know, however, that they brought an interpreter on board with them, a man called Luis Fernandez.

How strange to think that as *Hamlet* was being performed beneath the beating African sun by a raggedy crew of scurvy-stricken sailors, William Shakespeare was still alive and in the process of writing some of his finest plays.

That early performance of *Hamlet* on board the *Red Dragon* was the first of many Shakespeare productions to take place in Africa. In the twentieth century, Nelson Mandela famously described how Shakespeare had helped him survive the brutal conditions on Robben Island at the height of the struggle against apartheid. The late South African president described how he and his fellow prisoners would pass around a copy of the complete works of Shakespeare. In case any overzealous guards should confiscate the volume, they disguised it by pasting an image of a Hindu deity onto the cover. Mandela's favourite quote from the book came from the play *Julius Caesar*: 'Cowards die many times before their deaths, the valiant never taste of death but once.' Mandela remained in prison for twenty-seven years but drew hope from Shakespeare. So important was the volume to his sanity, it became known as the Robben Island Bible.

That homesick crew of the *Red Dragon* back in 1607 clearly appreciated Shakespeare too.

74. Apart from His Signatures Only One Example of His Handwriting Still Exists

For a man who spent so much of his time scribbling with a quill pen, we have precious few examples of Shakespeare's handwriting. Apart from six surviving signatures on various legal documents we don't have much to go on. He left no letters or diaries for eager scholars to pore over. One scrap of handwriting which has survived, however, can be found in the manuscript of the Elizabethan play *Sir Thomas More*. Written sometime before 1594, the play tells the story of Henry VIII's doomed chancellor. More was beheaded on Tower Hill in 1534 after refusing to accept the king as the head of the church in England. Some of the opening scenes are an adaptation of a real-life event in 1517 when the apprentices of London rioted against the presence of foreigners in the capital. On this 'Evil May Day' a mob of young men rampaged through the streets freeing prisoners, looting houses and attacking any foreigner unlucky enough to get in their way. At one point Thomas More, as under-sheriff of London, rode out to try and quell the violence. It is thought that it was Shakespeare who dramatised More's intervention in the play. He gives an impassioned defence of refugees:

> Imagine that you see the wretched strangers,
> Their babies at their backs and their poor luggage ...

Invoking the human fear of exile, he goes on:

> Say now the king (as he is clement, if th' offender mourn)
> Should so much come to short of your great trespass

As but to banish you, whither would you go?
What country, by the nature of your error, should
give you harbour?
Sir Thomas More, Act II, Scene IV

In real life More was unable to stop the rioting with pretty words. It was left to a troop of 5,000 guards who flooded the capital and seized prisoners. The ringleaders were taken to Westminster Hall to plead for their lives before the king. Ironically, it was a foreigner, Katherine of Aragon, who used her influence with Henry and ultimately prevented them from being executed.

The play *Sir Thomas More* is a superlative example of the Elizabethan practice of theatrical collaboration. The manuscript is a patchwork of writing with several hands detected. One of them is known as Hand D, the writer responsible for More's defence of the refugees. It is 'Hand D's' only contribution and is arguably the finest passage in the entire play, displaying Shakespeare's love of striking imagery and rhetoric. The handwriting has been analysed alongside his signatures and enough similarities found to convince scholars that our man was responsible.

Researchers have also put forward several other names as possible contributors, including Anthony Munday, Thomas Dekker, Henry Chettle and Thomas Heywood. If 'Hand D' is indeed Shakespeare, then not only does it show his humanity and empathy for struggling refugees, but it displays an early flash of brilliance in this writer who could only go from strength to strength.

75. His Daughter Judith Lived in a Cage

We saw earlier how Shakespeare's friend Richard Quiney wrote him a letter begging for a loan of £30 back in 1598. Eighteen years after the disastrous events in Stratford which had led Quiney to run up debts whilst staying in that tavern on Carter Lane, his son Thomas married Shakespeare's daughter Judith. It was an ill-starred marriage from the very beginning. The ceremony took place on 10 February 1616 during Lent, a period in which it was forbidden to marry unless you had a special licence from the ecclesiastical authorities. Thomas Quiney had not thought to furnish himself with one, for which crime he was briefly excommunicated by the Church.

That was not the worst of it. Two months after the marriage, a local woman named Margaret Wheeler died in childbirth. Her baby did not survive and they were buried together on 26 March. It was Thomas Quiney's child. In an age dominated by the Church, people who indulged in fornication and adultery could quickly find themselves publicly shamed. In this manner Quiney was hauled before the ecclesiastical Bawdy Court where he was sentenced to be paraded through the streets of Stratford under the disapproving gaze of his friends and neighbours. To add to his shame he would be dressed in a white sheet of penitence. Fortunately for Thomas, this degrading sentence was commuted and he was let off with a fine instead.

Married life could now begin. As a vintner and tobacconist he set up a tavern in the upper floor of a house on the corner of Stratford's High Street. This venue was known as The Cage after the prison which had formally been located in the cellar. His troubles continued when he was accused of selling contaminated wine and indulging in rowdy drinking sessions with his friends. His despairing father-in-law Shakespeare was probably in ill health by this time and beginning to worry about his daughter. What a lousy match she had made! It was around this time that Shakespeare made a decision about his will. The usual practice was for the man to take control of his wife's finances, so it was perhaps with this in mind that Shakespeare made provision in his will to his son-in-law. After the Margaret Wheeler debacle, however, he seems to have changed his mind, scrubbing out Quiney's name and adding his daughter's name instead. The document states that Judith was to receive her £100 marriage portion plus the interest on a further £150 to be paid three years after the date of the will.

Shakespeare had left his daughter a relatively well-off woman but it certainly looks as if he was washing his hands of her husband. That reprobate vintner fades into obscurity after this but it is believed he lived until 1663, passing the lease of The Cage on to his nephew. As for Judith, she died in 1662 at the excellent age of seventy-seven.

76. His Daughter Susannah Had Venereal Disease

If Judith Shakespeare had an unfortunate marriage to the womaniser Thomas Quiney, then Shakespeare's daughter Susannah made a much more fortunate match. In 1607 she married Stratford's only practicing doctor, the learned and upstanding Dr John Hall, a man of Puritan persuasions whose book of medical case studies went on the become a widely consulted reference book in the seventeenth century. He found his wife to be a willing guinea pig for his remedies, successfully treating Susannah for scurvy by giving her infusions made from watercress, citruses and berries rich in vitamin C. Scurvy was a common enough complaint in this period so Susannah must have counted her blessings to have had such a useful husband.

The couple lived quietly together in seeming tranquillity. John Hall enjoyed good relations with his father-in-law Shakespeare, even travelling down to London together on business. In 1608 they had a daughter Elizabeth and things were going well. Then one day their neat, ordered world was turned upside down.

Stratford was as religiously divided as anywhere else in seventeenth-century England. Broadly speaking the population comprised Anglicans, who adhered to the state religion, Catholics, and Puritans. Dr John Hall identified with the latter group and was a great supporter of Thomas Wilson, the Puritan vicar at Holy Trinity church. Having pulled down the town maypole, it is fair to say that Wilson was a divisive figure and he was the target of anti-Puritan riots upon his appointment in 1619. The mob broke the church windows and menaced the vicar with threats of violence. Hall's loyalty to the unpopular Wilson may have provoked an accusation which would cause Susannah much embarrassment.

In 1613, six years before Wilson became vicar of Holy Trinity, a local man called John Lane began spreading rumours. He told everyone that Susannah Hall, that respectable Puritan housewife, had been sleeping with the haberdasher Ralph Smith. Not only that, but her illicit liaison had resulted in her contracting a healthy dose of the clap. John Lane sneeringly accused her of having venereal disease. It wasn't true but an accusation such as this would cause scandal among the townsfolk. Who would want to be seen in company with the doctor's wife now? It could have caused irreparable damage to Hall's medical practice. Furious, the couple took their grievance to court, suing John Lane for defamation. Their brave accuser failed to show up and defend his actions. Unsurprisingly the case was thrown out and Lane was excommunicated for his troubles. Susannah was clearly not one to be messed with.

In later years her daughter Elizabeth married Thomas Nash, a supporter of the Royalists in the civil War. Elizabeth and Thomas hosted Queen Henrietta Maria during the war at New Place, the grand manor house which Shakespeare had bought back in 1597. By the time of the queen's visit in 1643, John Hall was dead so we will never know how that Puritan gentleman would have reacted to the Catholic queen's visit.

77. He Once Lived in a Monastery

The area of London known as Blackfriars takes its name from the monastery which once stood upon the site. The Dominican monks were often called the Black Friars, owing to the black habits they wore. They founded their religious house in 1221 and would remain there, praying and chanting in peace, right up until 1538 when their luck ran out. By this time Henry VIII was on the throne and he was in the process of separating the English church from Rome. As part of the process he dissolved all the religious houses one by one. Before the Blackfriars monastery fell, it played its part in one of the most dramatic moments of Henry's reign when a trial was held there to test the validity of his marriage to his first wife Katherine of Aragon. Henry thought he could use the hearing to convince the public that his marriage had been invalid owing to her prior marriage to his late brother Arthur. It was to be a public humiliation. Sadly for the king, Katherine was to prove far wilier than he imagined and was able to turn the tables on her husband by delivering a speech which was worthy of the great Shakespeare himself. She argued that she had been a virgin upon her marriage to Henry, and was therefore his legal wife.

With so much drama happening in such a small area is it any wonder that we find Shakespeare turning up? In 1613 Shakespeare purchased the gatehouse of the old monastery. Built above the eastern entrance to the site, it would have proven an ideal location – not only was it a short wherry ride away from the Globe on Bankside, it was also close to the indoor playhouse where the King's Men regularly performed. The playhouse was located in the old monks' refectory and it was here that the company later re-enacted a version of Katherine of Aragon's passionate speech in the play *Henry VIII*:

> Sir, I desire you do me right and justice;
> And to bestow your pity on me: for
> I am a most poor woman, and a stranger,
> Born out of your dominions; having here
> No judge indifferent, nor no more assurance
> Of equal friendship and proceeding. Alas sir,
> In what have I offended you?
> Queen Katherine, *Henry VIII*, Act II, Scene IV

How strange to think that Katherine's haunting words should have echoed through that space once more.

Some scholars have used Shakespeare's monastical choice of location when purchasing property as proof that he was a secret Catholic. Bearing in mind that by this time England had broken away from Rome and embraced Protestantism, there was a strong underground Catholic movement. Shakespeare's gatehouse was located next door to the scene of an illegal Catholic mass which took place in 1623 at the French Ambassador's house. Over 300 people were gathered in a room at the top of the building when the floor collapsed killing over ninety people. It was thereafter known as the Doleful Evensong.

78. If You Ever Asked Shakespeare Out for a Drink He Would Pretend to Have Tummy Ache

If you think that life in Early Modern London was all prayers and religious squabbles, think again. A letter written by the playwright Francis Beaumont to his colleague Ben Jonson paints a vivid portrait of the fun to be had in the local drinking holes. Beaumont waxes lyrical about one establishment in particular, the Mermaid Tavern on Bread Street. Here he is reminiscing about the evenings spent drinking and exchanging witty banter with Jonson:

> What things have we seen
> Done at the Mermaid? Heard words that have been
> So nimble, and so full of subtle flame,
> As if that every one from whence they came,
> Had meant to put his whole wit in a jest,
> And had resolved to live a fool the rest of his dull life.

You can see it now; a shadowy tavern, dimly illuminated by flickering candlelight; a group of men crowd over a beer-soaked table as they slur sozzled witticisms at one another. It sounds like a typical Friday night at the Dog and Duck, and Shakespeare, too, could have been among the company. The landlord of the Mermaid was a man named William Johnson who had witnessed Shakespeare's mortgage on the Blackfriars gatehouse in 1613. Johnson is said to have kept a quiet, orderly tavern, banning music and gambling. He was less successful at preventing disorder spilling out from his tavern and into the city streets, however. An interesting case from 1600 when Edmund Baynham and his group of rabble rousers left the Mermaid at midnight and went marching through London with daggers and rapiers drawn. After attacking the night-watchmen, Bayham was arrested, crying out defiantly that 'he cared not a fart for the Lord Mayor or any magistrate in London'.

Whether Shakespeare was such a heavy drinker is doubtful. Indeed an anecdote from John Aubrey in 1681 claims that Shakespeare was more likely than not to turn down any invitation to a night of fun. Aubrey writes that Shakespeare 'would not be debauched. If invited to, he writ he was in pain'. Aubrey got this gossip from the son of Shakespeare's colleague Kit Beeston so it has an air of authenticity about it. Who can blame him if he claimed the odd headache or sore belly? Plays didn't write themselves, after all.

There is a strong sense that Shakespeare was a man who held back slightly from the crowd. He was the quiet one in the corner, observing people and their behaviour, perhaps making notes and scribbling down scraps of overheard conversation. He certainly set some of his most authentic scenes in taverns. Take the Boar's Head on Eastcheap, which featured in some of the comic scenes of the plays of *Henry IV*. This is Falstaff's favourite hangout, that sack soaked old lush. In the play *Henry V*, a war weary boy says wistfully, 'I would give all my fame for a pot of ale.' Shakespeare may not have enjoyed it himself but it seems his characters loved a tipple.

79. He Annoyed a Grumpy Vicar

In 1597 Shakespeare joined the ranks of the Stratford glitterati when he bought New Place, the second largest house in town. Located on the corner of Chapel Street and Chapel Lane, opposite the Guild Chapel, it was a huge five gabled structure with extensive grounds. It had been built by Hugh Clopton, a wealthy mercer, in 1483 and was one of the first buildings in Stratford to be made of brick rather than timber. After purchasing it for £60 – a huge sum – Shakespeare moved his family out of Henley Street and into their glamorous new abode.

He may not have spent much time at New Place himself; at this point he was still based in London, churning out a steady stream of plays whilst trying to swerve invites to the Mermaid Tavern. It is thought he made only made annual visits home to Stratford, perhaps staying for a month or so, but he finally retired to New Place in 1614. The London days were over. For the final two years of his life he may have taken a deep breath and allowed the stresses of work to melt away as he enjoyed his retirements in the rolling Warwickshire countryside.

Upon his death in 1616 the house passed into the ownership of John and Susannah Hall, who in turn bequeathed it to their daughter Elizabeth. When Elizabeth died in 1670 the house reverted to Clopton ownership before finally falling into the hands of a rather grumpy vicar.

By the middle of the eighteenth century a fledgling Shakespeare tourist trail had developed, with visitors from all over the country making pilgrimage to Stratford. Obvious points of attraction were Shakespeare's birthplace on Henley Street, his memorial at Holy Trinity Church, and the home of the Reverend Francis Gastrell, who had the misfortune of living in New Place. The house had been redeveloped and enlarged by Gastrell's residence but it was still an integral part of the Shakespeare story. It attracted hordes of visitors who invaded his privacy by going into the garden and taking samples from an old mulberry tree believed to have been planted by Shakespeare himself. In exasperation he had the tree cut down, selling it to a man who turned a coin by carving souvenirs from the wood. The story does not end there, however. The locals were so infuriated at the loss of the tree that they attacked Gastrell's house, at which point the unfortunate Reverend must have been cursing the name William Shakespeare. He had one more trick up his sleeve, and in 1759 he knocked the house down, reducing Shakespeare's pride and joy to a pile of rubble. For this act of iconoclasm, he was driven out of town.

A major archaeological project has recently been undertaken at New Place, uncovering various artefacts dating from Shakespeare's residence in the house. The Shakespeare Birthplace Trust plans to open the site to visitors in time for Shakespeare's birthday in 2016, bringing his world to life once more.

80. He Lost His Seal Ring in the Garden

In 1810 a Stratford historian named Robert Bell Wheler made an exciting purchase. Mrs Martin, a local woman, had stumbled upon an old ring whilst labouring in the fields near Holy Trinity church. It was solid gold and bore the initials 'W S'. Winding its way through these initials was a love knot. Wheler's immediate thought was that the 'W S' stood for William Shakespeare and he swiftly arranged to take it off Mrs Martin's hands. He told the story of what happened in his 1814 guide to Stratford.

According to Wheler the ring 'had undoubtedly been lost a great many years, being nearly black; and though it was purchased upon the same day for thirty-six shillings (the current value of gold) the woman had sufficient time to destroy the precious patina by consenting to have it unnecessarily immersed in aquafortis'. Mrs Martin may not have realised that acid was harmful to gold and silver but no real harm was done. With strong suspicions that this was Shakespeare's ring, Wheler consulted the scholar Edmund Malone who 'said he had nothing to allege against the probability of my conjecture as to its owner'.

Wheler went on to speculate about how Shakespeare had come to lose the ring as well as how he come to acquire it, deciding that it was his wedding ring. In the breathy tones of a bodice-ripping novelist he wrote: 'William kissed his bride with all the tenderness of pure and ardent young love and then placed upon her finger a gold ring. "Keep this remembrance for my sake," he may have said to his young bride.' In Wheler's fantasy, Anne then slipped the ring with its 'W S' initials onto William's finger.

The ring in question was a seal ring of the type used by gentlemen, especially businessmen, in the sixteenth and seventeenth centuries. If this was indeed Shakespeare's ring he would have used it to seal up his correspondences while, at the same time, identifying himself as the sender. After dipping the ring in warm wax and stamping it upon the folded letter, the initals W S would have been visible to the recipient. Like the ardent Shakespeare fan Wheler, we still speculate as to how he lost it. One compelling theory put forward by scholars is that Shakespeare lost it in 1616 on the day of his daughter's wedding at Holy Trinity church. Bearing in mind that the ring was found close to the church, this is quite plausible. Shakespeare was probably ailing at the time of Judith's wedding. Shortly afterwards he signed his will with the words 'whereunto I put my hand and seal'. The word 'seal' is crossed out.

Shakespeare's seal ring is now held by the Shakespeare Birthplace Trust, having been given it by Wheler's sister after his death. It would be interesting to know whether its finder Mrs Martin knew about the Shakespeare connection. In any case, let's hope she enjoyed her thirty-six shillings. After such a find, she surely deserved more.

81. SHAKESPEARE WAS ALWAYS SUING HIS NEIGHBOURS

We have seen that the Reverend Francis Gastrell was a grumpy neighbour but it could also be argued that Shakespeare was too. Over his lifetime he found himself involved in various court actions. Let us have a look at some of them:

Shakespeare versus Edmund Lambert: Many of us have tangled family relations and the Shakespeare family was no exception. The roots to this particular dispute begin in 1580 when John Shakespeare, the poet's father, borrowed £40 from his brother-in-law Edmund Lambert. As security, John mortgaged forty-four acres of land at Wilmcote. This was his wife Mary Arden's inheritance so the decision would not have been taken lightly. At the end of the agreed term John tried to pay Lambert the £40, but in the meantime he had accrued further debts, so his shrewd brother-in-law refused to give up the land. John Shakespeare took him to court and the case dragged on until 1597, when William Shakespeare took control of the dispute and took it to the Court of Chancery. He had no luck there – the court merely ticked him off for wasting court time with frivolous suits. We have no record of the ultimate outcome.

Shakespeare versus Philip Rogers: This is an interesting case. In the Elizabethan era crop failure was a serious issue. It could mean life or death for those too poor to have their own stores of grain or malt. In a worthy attempt to address the issue, Elizabeth I banned the practice of hoarding grain and decreed that anything beyond that needed for ordinary household use should be sold on. Not everyone adhered to the regulations. The late Elizabethan years were a time of great food insecurity, as we saw in 1598 when famine forced Richard Quiney to beg for relief in London. One of those hoarding grain in 1598 was William Shakespeare and he was prosecuted for the crime. By 1604 it appears he was still at it. That year, he had the audacity to sue his neighbour Philip Rogers for an unpaid bill on some bushels of malt he had sold him. It was not just a handful of malt Shakespeare had sold his neighbour, it was twenty bushels. He had no legitimate reason to be hoarding such a vast amount. Nevertheless, Roger was two shillings down on his repayments so Shakespeare took him to court. The poet also asked for ten shillings to defray his expenses, whatever they may have been.

Shakespeare versus John Addenbrooke: In 1608 Shakespeare sued his neighbour John Addenbrooke for a debt of £6. The case dragged on for ten months during which time Addenbrooke was arrested. At some point Addenbrooke broke bail so Shakespeare pursued his guarantor Thomas Hornby for the unpaid debt. We have no record of whether or not he was ever paid.

Shakespeare versus Stratford: This was a joint action in 1609. Shakespeare had invested in shares of the Stratford tithes and, following a squabble about who needed to pay what, he took the case to court.

82. SHAKESPEARE WROTE MASQUES, BUT NOT FOR COURT

As well as plays being performed at the public playhouses, there was another type of drama doing the rounds in the Early Modern period. The court masque was an elevated form of entertainment aimed not at the popular rabble to be found at the Globe, but squarely at noble and aristocratic audiences. Not only was the audience drawn from the upper classes, but so was the cast. Unlike public performances at the playhouse, women played a full role in the drama, which normally took place in a purpose built banqueting house at Whitehall.

The first Banqueting House was built by Elizabeth I in preparation for the visit of her suitor the Duc'd'Alencon who visited in 1581. It was little more than a wooden frame draped with brightly painted canvas and was as impermanent as her changeable moods. It was James I who built something more lasting. He did not like Whitehall with its warren-like maze of alleyways and dead ends. In 1606 he decided to start afresh and commissioned a new design with clean, rectilinear lines and open spaces. At the same time he added the Banqueting House, a building which still exists today. The Venetian ambassador described it as, 'a large hall fitted up like a theatre, with well secured boxes all around. The stage is at one end, and his majesty's chair in front under an ample canopy.' It was here that James would enjoy a performance of *The Tempest* by The King's Men on 1 November 1611. The play was performed again two years later to celebrate the marriage of the Lady Elizabeth to Frederick, Elector Palatine of Bohemia. *The Tempest* is a strange, ethereal play full of music and magic. The royal couple would have enjoyed the masque scene Shakespeare inserted – perhaps with their marriage in mind:

> Juno: How does my bounteous sister? Go with me
> To bless this twain, that they may prosperous be
> And honour'd in their issue.
> (They sing)
> Juno: Honour, riches, marriage-blessing,
> Hourly joys be still upon you!
> Juno sings her blessings upon you.
> (*The Tempest*, Act IV, Scene I)

In this scene Prospero has called forth his spirits to perform an entertainment for Miranda and Ferdinand who are newly betrothed. What follows is a classic example of the type of courtly masque performed by, and for, royals and aristocracy. These entertainments were characterised by the liberal use of music, poetry and dance. It was a very visual form of theatre with professionally designed scenery and elaborate costumes. An example is Ben Jonson's *Masque of Blackness* which was commissioned by Anne of Denmark and performed at the Banqueting House on Twelfth Night, 1605.

It is interesting to note that despite his friend Ben Jonson's involvement in masques, Shakespeare seemed to have no interest them himself. He may have inserted a masque scene into *The Tempest* but there is no record of him ever writing a full length masque to be performed at court. It is hard to believe he was never asked.

83. He Based Prospero on Himself

Speaking of *The Tempest*, there are some critics who believe that Shakespeare had someone in particular in mind when he created the character of Prospero – himself.

It is easy to see why. After all, Prospero has immense magical powers and so did Shakespeare (if you are willing to compare Shakespeare's talent to magic). If we have a look at Prospero's role in *The Tempest*, we may be able to judge whether or not Shakespeare was writing about himself.

Our friendly magician has always had an interest in magic, locking himself away for hours to study the art. Eventually his brother exiles him and his daughter Miranda to a remote island inhabited by spirits where they remain for twelve years. Meanwhile his brother Alonso has usurped his dukedom and is living the high life in Milan. Not wishing to stand for this, Prospero uses his magic skills to whip up a huge storm and sink his brother's ship. Alonso survives and swims to the island where a vengeful Prospero awaits. After various adventures including Ferdinand's wooing of Miranda and the young couple's betrothal, Prospero decides it is time for a quiet life and drops several hints about renouncing his magic powers:

> But this rough magic
> I here abjure, and, when I have requir'd
> Some heavenly music, which even now I do,
> To work mine end upon their senses that
> This airy charm is for, I'll break my staff,
> Bury it certain fathoms in the earth,

And deeper than did ever plummet sounds,
I'll drown my book.
(*The Tempest*, Act V, Scene I)

All this talk of 'breaking staffs' and 'drowning books' sounds like somebody who wants to give up all the power he has gained through study and become a mere mortal once again. Perhaps Shakespeare saw a parallel between the art of magic and the art of bringing stories alive on stage through poetry. *The Tempest* was probably written in 1611 when Shakespeare's output was beginning to decline. Indeed, it would be the last play he ever wrote alone. As we saw earlier, the play *Henry VIII* came later but that was a collaborative effort with John Fletcher. He even goes on to make what seems to be a farewell to the Globe and all the actors within it:

You do look, my son, in a moved sort,
As if you were dismay'd: be cheerful, sir.
Our revels now are ended. These our actors,
As I foretold you, were all spirits and
Are melted into air, into thin air:
And like the baseless fabric of this vision,
The cloud-capp'd towers, the gorgeous palaces,
The solemn temples, the great globe itself,
Yea, all which it inherit, shall dissolve,
And like this insubstantial pageant faded,
Leave not a rack behind ...
The Tempest, Act IV, Scene I

If Shakespeare is talking about the end of his own career, and not just that of Prospero, then this is a doubly poignant speech. By this time he may have been yearning to go home to Stratford.

84. In 1616 He Had the Worst Birthday Present Ever – He Died

Not long after Shakespeare wrote *The Tempest*, he did indeed 'break his staff' and 'drown his books'. He is believed to have retired in 1614 and ridden back to Stratford for the final time. We have no way of knowing how he might have felt about leaving London; perhaps he was happy to finally stop the backbreaking work of bending over a desk by candlelight and churning out a never-ending supply of plays. Perhaps by this point his eyesight was fading and he was finding the task more and more difficult. Of course, there is always the possibility that he rode home to Stratford fully intending to return to London and resume his career with the King's Men. Whatever the circumstances of his retirement, it was the end of an era. He was now free to spend some quality time in his fine mansion New Place, and indeed spend some time with his wife Anne. For a couple who had lived apart from each other for so long it may have been quite an adjustment and it is easy to imagine a crabby Shakespeare wandering from room to room, not knowing what to do with all this spare time.

As it turned out, he did not have much time left to spare. On 23 April 1616 he died. It was his birthday, which was unfortunate timing indeed, but it appears that he had, at least, been enjoying himself that week. There is an interesting legend about how his demise came about, one which involves a lot of boozing with old friends. If we are to believe John Ward, a Stratford vicar, the playwright's end may have been hastened when 'Shakespeare, Drayton, and Ben Jonson had a merry meeting, and it seems drank too much, for Shakespeare died of a fever there contracted.'

Ward was born thirteen years after Shakespeare's death so could not possibly have got this gossip at first hand. It would be interesting to know who told him. As we have seen, quite a few of the stories about Shakespeare's life come from gossip passed down the generations and although this can never be completely reliable (think Chinese whispers), it would be a shame to discount it altogether.

Shakespeare was fifty-two years old when he died. From a distance of 400 years it sounds too cruel to die so young but it was in fact a good age for a man born in the sixteenth century. The average lifespan for an Elizabethan man was only forty-two and most people would be lucky to reach such a grand age. The Grim Reaper's scythe was a constant presence. If you were lucky enough to survive childhood then the plague might get you, or a difficult childbirth, or starvation caused by crop failure, or, if you were really unfortunate, you might be hung for stealing a loaf of bread.

A wealthy man like Shakespeare was insulated from most of these hazards but there was no cure for a heavy night's drinking.

85. Anyone Who Moves His Bones Will Be Cursed Forever

Two days after Shakespeare's death he was put to rest in the chancel of his local church Holy Trinity. Just feet away from his burial place is the font in which he had been baptised fifty-two years earlier. It was a privilege to be buried in the chancel. Shakespeare had earned this right as a sharcholder of the Stratford tithes (a form of local tax) and this was also extended to members of his family. In this way, he was later joined in death by his wife Anne Hathaway, their daughter Susannah, her husband Dr John Hall, and Thomas Nash, the first husband of Susannah's daughter Elizabeth.

It was quite the family reunion. It would appear, however, that Shakespeare did not feel entirely secure in his resting place. Engraved on his tomb is a curse designed to scare off any grave diggers. It is thought that Shakespeare wrote these words himself:

> Good friend for Jesus' sake forbear
> To dig the dust enclosed here.
> Blessed be the man that spares these stones,
> And cursed be he that moves my bones.

So far nobody has dared to defy him but it can only be a matter of time before some inquisitive soul asks for permission to dig him up. What can Shakespeare have been worried about? After all, it was hardly likely that his remains would be disturbed, especially with the privileged position he enjoyed in Stratford society. In fact, as far as Shakespeare was concerned, there was always a small risk that he might be shifted to make room for someone else. In the springtime of

1616 as his life began to ebb away, he could not have known that posterity would treasure his memory to the extent it does. The idea of a Shakespeare industry would have been quite alien to him. With burial space at a premium it would have been quite reasonable for him to assume his bones might be moved. He had seen it happen to others, after all. Not far from the chancel at Holy Trinity was a large charnel house. When the bodies buried outside in the graveyard became too numerous, it was common practice to disinter them to make way for new arrivals. The old bones would then be stored in the charnel house. This repository of human remains seems to have held a dark fascination for Shakespeare. He refers to it in Act IV, Scene I of *Romeo and Juliet* among a list of things Juliet would rather do than get married to Paris:

> ... Or shut me nightly in a charnel house,
> O'er covered quite with dead men's rattling bones,
> With reeky shanks and yellow chapless skulls.

Paris must have been quite a catch ...

Juliet's horror at the idea of spending a night in the charnel house gives us an idea of the power it must have held over the local imagination. Shakespeare's fears about becoming one of its inhabitants were unfounded in the end. The curse must have worked.

86. The Bust of Shakespeare in Holy Trinity Church Originally Had Him Holding a Bag of Grain Rather than a Quill

Shakespeare's place in the chancel was quickly consolidated with a memorial bust in his honour. His fellow poet Leonard Digges refers to it in some commendatory lines to Shakespeare in the First Folio: 'When that stone is rent, and time dissolves thy Stratford monument, here we alive shall view thee still.' The Folio was published in 1623, meaning that Shakespeare's monument must have sprung up within a few years after his death, the news of it travelling all the way to London.

It is likely to have been Anne Hathaway who oversaw the work, maybe even commissioning it herself as a lasting tribute to her late husband. Placed in a niche in the north wall of the chancel, the bust shows Shakespeare sitting between two blue classical columns. He wears a dark cloak over a red doublet, his white collar poking out as it does in the Chandos portrait. There is also that familiar domed forehead and receding hairline. He stares sightlessly ahead, a piece of paper in one hand and a quill pen in the other. It has to be said this is not the most flattering portrait of the Bard. This is no dashing, poetic hero. He has been described as having the air of a 'self-satisfied pork butcher'. Nevertheless, Anne Hathaway is said to have approved of its likeness to her husband.

A plaque beneath the bust offers the following tribute:

Stay, passenger, why goest thou by so fast?
Read, if thou canst, whom envious death hath placed

Within this monument: Shakespeare with whom
Quick nature died; whose name doth deck his tomb
For more than cost; sith all that he had writ
Leaves living art but page to serve his wit.

The artist was a Dutchman named Gerard Johnson who spent some time working in England during the second decade of the seventeenth century. Appropriately enough for someone with a history of hoarding food, some believe that Shakespeare was originally depicted holding a bag of grain instead of a quill. This theory almost certainly derives from a seventeenth-century engraving of the memorial bust by Sir William Dugdale whose drawing made the cushion Shakespeare leans upon to appear more bulky than it actually is. Conspiracy theorists sometimes suggest that it represented a sack of grain and hold it as proof that William Shakespeare of Stratford was a grain dealer rather than a playwright. In fact, it is tells us more about Dugdale's drawing skills than Shakespeare's playwright career.

The quill itself has been stolen many times over the years. The monument has also been repainted a few times since its creation; at one point it was painted entirely white at the instigation of Edmund Malone who thought a classical veneer would be more appropriate than the multicoloured original.

Today the monument is colourful once more and attracts scores of visitors who flock to Holy Trinity in their thousands to pay their respects to Shakespeare.

87. He Was a Mean Curmudgeon Who Ignored His Wife and Left Her the 'Second-Best Bed' in His Will

One of the charges often levelled at Shakespeare is that he did not care much for his wife Anne Hathaway. Critics suggest that the seven-year age gap between the pair as well as their hurried marriage indicate that, perhaps, Shakespeare might have preferred to have married someone else. Perhaps his true love was the mysterious Anne Whateley, or the London ladies Lucy Morgan and Emelia Lanier. We are also reminded of the fact that it was two of Anne's kinsmen who travelled to Worcester to get the wedding license. Does this indicate that the young eighteen-year-old Shakespeare had been forced into marriage after a bit of harvest-time fun left Anne Hathaway pregnant? After all, he spent most of his working life separated from her. There is no record of Anne ever following her husband down to London or even visiting him there. It is usually assumed that they were reunited annually on Shakespeare's visits home.

There is something else which sometimes gives rise to suspicion about Shakespeare's love – or lack of – for Anne. He signed his will on 25 March 1616, in the presence of his lawyer Francis Collins, just one month before he died. The will begins with a preamble in which he makes the usual claim to be of sound mind and aware of what he is signing:

In the name of God Amen, I William Shackspeare of Stratford upon Avon in the country of Warwickshire, gent; in perfect health and memory God be praised, do make and ordain this my last will and testament in manner and form following.

He goes on to commend his soul to God before getting down to the nitty gritty. To his old colleagues in the King's Men, John Heminges and Henry Condell, Shakespeare left money to buy themselves memorial rings. His sister Joan received the sum of £20 plus the right to stay in the house on Henley Street for the rest of her life. He left his mansion New Place to his daughter Susannah with the proviso that it would pass down the line of her heirs. To his wife Anne, he left the 'second-best bed'. It is an extraordinarily specific bequest and on the face of it seems like a snub. Why could she not have the best bed? She was his wife, after all. Before we get too indignant on Anne's behalf, however, it is worth considering that the best bed in a Jacobean household would normally be used to accommodate any visitors. Beds were an item of luxury and it was usual to display them in the living quarters for visitors to admire. Visitors to the Shakespeare Birthplace on Henley Street can see an example of this where a replica four-poster is displayed downstairs. The second-best bed would be located in the man and wife's private chamber.

In Shakespeare's defence, therefore, it can be assumed that his bequest to Anne was not so much a snub as a reminder of their affection for one another.

88. HE DIDN'T PUBLISH HIS PLAYS HIMSELF – HE LEFT THAT TO HIS FRIENDS

Shakespeare did not seem too bothered about seeing his plays in print but his friends certainly were. Seven years after his death a collection of his tragedies, histories and comedies was released to a ravenous public. The First Folio, as it is known, brought together all of his work into one volume allowing his genius to live on in the memories of those who had been lucky enough to see his original productions.

The compilers of this remarkable book were two men who Shakespeare had known well. John Heminges and Henry Condell were his fellow King's Men actors and shareholders at the Globe. They lived in the parish of Aldermanbury and served as church wardens at the parish church of St Mary's. From 1604 onwards, when Shakespeare lived around the corner on Silver Street with the Mountjoy family, it would have been easy for the three of them to meet up during their time off. They must have been fairly close friends for Shakespeare to have left them money in his will to buy their memorial rings. What happened to the rings is a mystery but, in any case, Heminges and Condell had a more permanent memorial in mind and set about creating the First Folio. It seems their intention was to safeguard Shakespeare's reputation, which was constantly being undermined by the publication of inferior copies of his plays. In a gushing preface they described the dead man's plays as 'orphans' and said their intention was 'only to keep the memory of so worthy a friend, and fellow alive, as was our Shakespeare, by humble offer of his plays to your most noble patronage'. However much they had loved their dear Shakespeare, they were clearly keen to shift copies and not afraid to try a sales pitch. Addressing the general public they wrote: 'Well! It [the book] is now public and you will stand for your privileges we know: to read and censure. Do so, but buy it first. That doth best commend a book, the Stationer says. Then, how odd soever your brains be, or your wisdoms, make your license the same and spare not ... but whatever you do, buy.' Considering that the price of the book was £1 (a huge sum for the average Jacobean Londoner), Heminges and Condell were right to try and drum up trade.

They dedicated the folio to William Herbert, 3rd Earl of Pembroke, believed by some to be the 'lovely boy' of the sonnets. Along with the preface written by Heminges and Condell the folio included a number of dedicatory poems to Shakespeare written by his friends and acquaintances. One of the loveliest was by Ben Jonson who described his old pal as the 'sweet swan of Avon' in a reference to his Warwickshire roots. In 1616 Jonson published a folio of his own work, perhaps with an eye on posterity. Shakespeare was much more modest and never showed an interest in seeing his own work in print, but posterity treasures him more.

89. THE FIRST FOLIO IS ALWAYS BEING STOLEN

It is strange to think that if Heminges and Condell had not compiled the First Folio a great deal of Shakespeare's plays would have been lost for eternity. Generations of schoolchildren may have cursed the duo for saving the likes of *Julius Caesar* and *Macbeth*, but it is a good job that they did. The Great Fire of London was just around the corner; it was a devastating blaze which wiped out most of medieval London and had the potential to erase any surviving Shakespeare quartos which may have been gathering dust on people's bookshelves. Considering the wordiness of Shakespeare's plays, the work involved in compiling the folio would have been immense. It is true that as members of the King's Men, Heminges and Condell had unique access to the scripts used in rehearsals as well as the familiarity bred by acting in those plays day in, day out. Elizabethan and Jacobean culture was very aural and people were used to soaking up huge amounts of information just by listening. The short attention span that characterises the twenty-first century was a long way off yet.

Nobody is entirely sure how many copies of the First Folio were printed but it is sometimes estimated to be approximately 1,000. Of these, just over 200 are left in existence, most of them in the Folger Library, Washington DC, and it is fair to say they command a far higher price than they did in 1623, attracting million-pound price tags on the rare occasion they come up for sale. As a primary source for scholars of Shakespeare's work, its worth cannot be overestimated. For such a valuable product, it is no surprise that the folio has been stolen a few times.

One of the most intriguing thefts took place in 1998 when a first folio was swiped from Durham University. Nobody knew what had become of it; it had seemingly vanished into thin air. Ten long years passed before a man named Raymond Scott walked into the Folger Library and asked staff to take a look at an old book he had in his possession. He told them that a friend had given it to him in Cuba. Shocked staff realised it was a Shakespeare First Folio, and suspicious of the man's story, they called in the FBI. It was identified as the copy stolen from Durham University ten years earlier and Scott was jailed. Incredibly, security at the library was so lax that Scott had managed to take the copy from a filing cabinet with little more than a screwdriver. He later took his own life in Northumberland Prison.

In another case of theft, a copy was taken from Williams College in Massachusetts only to be returned the following year because the thief could not sell it. With so few folios in existence, their individual features are all well documented, making it practically impossible to sell a stolen copy on the open market.

The First Folio can be viewed at the British Library – but leave the screwdriver at home!

90. Ben Jonson Was His Most Critical Friend

In 1640 Ben Jonson was in nostalgic mood. Most of the Elizabethan actors and playwrights he had worked with were long dead, Shakespeare included. He decided to publish his memories of Shakespeare; they are very illuminating about the characters of both men. Jonson begins with an anecdote about how the actors had praised Shakespeare for the ease with which he knocked out his plays. He only needed one draft to get it right:

> I remember the players have often mentioned it as an honour to Shakespeare, that in his writing, whatsoever he penned, he never blotted out a line. My answer hath been "Would he had blotted a thousand," which they thought a malevolent speech.

The scene is easy to imagine; a sniffy Ben Jonson contradicting the praise being heaped on his late rival – well, he may not have scrapped any of his lines out but he jolly well should have done! The indignant players who rounded on Jonson for his 'malevolence' must have been fond of Shakespeare indeed. Jonson was quick to defend his motives. He loved Shakespeare really – even if he did ramble on a bit too much sometimes:

> I had not told posterity this but for their ignorance, who chose that circumstance to commend their friend by wherein he most faulted; and to justify mine own candour, for I loved the man, and do honour his memory on this side idolatry as much as any. He was, indeed honest, and of an open and free nature; had an

excellent fancy, brave notions, and gentle expressions, wherein he flowed with that facility that sometime it was necessary he should be stopped ... his wit was in his own power; would the rule of it had been so too.

Jonson also hints at the laugher they shared. In this anecdote he mocks Shakespeare's use of poetic meter in the play *Julius Caesar*.

Many times he fell into those things, could not escape laughter, as when he said in the person of Caesar, one speaking to him: 'Caesar, thou dost me wrong.' He replied, 'Caesar never did wrong but with just cause', and such like, which were ridiculous. But he redeemed his vices with his virtues. There was ever more in him to be praised than to be pardoned.

Shakespeare must have taken his criticism to heart because the line was changed to 'Know, Caesar doth not wrong, nor without cause will he be satisfied.' It seems that Shakespeare and Jonson enjoyed a lively, if sometimes combative relationship. A seventeenth-century writer claimed to have seen them lock horns at the Mermaid Tavern:

Many were the wit combats betwixt him and Ben Jonson which two I behold like a Spanish great galleon and an English man-of-war. Master Jonson, (like the former) was built far higher in learning; solid, but slow in his performances. Shakespeare, lesser in bulk but lighter in sailing could turn with all tides ... by the quickness of his wit and invention.

No prizes for guessing who won.

91. THE LONGEST WORD IN SHAKESPEARE IS 'HONORIFICABILITUNDINITATIBUS'

Maybe Ben Jonson should not have been so quick to dismiss Shakespeare as having 'small Latin and little Greek'. Clever clogs Jonson, with all his learning, never once managed to use the word *honorificabilitundinatibus* in any of his works. Shakespeare did, in the play *Love's Labour's Lost*. The word trips off Costard's tongue as easily as if it were the commonest thing for a Shakespearean clown to say. Here is Costard – or Shakespeare, perhaps – showing off his Latin:

Moth (Aside to Costard): They have been at a great feast of languages, and stolen the scraps.
Costard: O, they have lived long on the alms-basket of words. I marvel thy master hath not eaten thee for a word; for thou art not so long by the head as honorificabilitudinitatibus: thou art easier swallowed than a flap-dragon.

Love's Labour's Lost, Act V, Scene I

It is easy to imagine the original actor who spoke these lines pausing for dramatic effect after that horrifically long word before pretending it was a piece of cake, actually. 'Thou art easier swallowed than a flap-dragon.' A flap-dragon was a raisin soaked in burning brandy. On Christmas Eve it was traditional to boil the brandy in a bowl along with some raisins which would be set on fire; the revellers would have to try and eat them without getting burnt. In the above scene, before Costard's speech, Holofernes, Sir Nathaniel, and Dull had been making fun of Armado's overblown speech patterns and also trying out their Latin on each other.

Shakespeare did not use much Latin in his plays generally and, compared the pretentious gentlemen in *Love's Labour's Lost*, he kept his language simple. If only Holofernes could have done the same:

> Holofernes: He draweth out the thread of his verbosity finer than the staple of his argument. I abhor such fanatical phantasimes, such insociable and point-devise companions; such rackers of orthography, as to speak dout, fine, when he should say doubt; det, when he should pronounce debt – d,e,b,t, not d,e,t: he clepeth a calf, cauf; half, hauf ...

Audiences would have been aware that Shakespeare was mocking, especially when Costard arrived and said 'honoricabilitudinitatibus'.

Of course, all you Latin lovers out there will know that the word honoricabilitudinitatibus comes from the plural of honorificabilitudinitas. You didn't know that? Well, let's allow the Collins English Dictionary to explain. It gives the definition as 'invincible glorious honourableness. It is the ablative plural of the Latin contrived honorificabilitudinitas, which is an extension of honorificabilis meaning honorableness.' Of course, we all knew that really. The context in which Costard uses the word is nonsense. He is just showing off. Nevertheless, the word had been heard in rarified circles since the Middle Ages, for example in the thirteenth century when an English scholar, Gervase of Melkley, made use of it in a treatise on rhetoric. Neither was Shakespeare the only playwright to say honoricabilitudinitatibus; his colleague John Marston used it in *The Dutch Courtesan* of 1605.

92. The King's Men's Careers Ended in Arrest

When James I died the King's Men's patronage was transferred to his son, Charles I. This period saw a boom in the building of indoor playhouses to rival the Blackfriars; Richard Gunnell, a veteran of the Admiral's Men, built the indoor Salisbury Court just outside the western boundary of the city walls, not far from the Blackfriars. Further west, on a site near Drury Lane, was the Cockpit. This was to be the first playhouse in what we know as the West End, a pioneer in this new territory. Up until now, the theatre scene had been confined to small patches of land on Bankside, in Shoreditch and at the Blackfriars Playhouse. When the fields to the west of the city began to be developed in the seventeenth century, London's entertainment centre gradually followed, shifting to what would become a playground for the rich and the fashionable.

The Puritans closed the theatres in 1642, but far from hanging up their costumes, the King's Men continued to stage the occasional illicit performance. This was a company which had evolved over a period of fifty years, surviving the turbulent political landscape of three different monarchs. Now, the hourglass was running out and it not be long before a shameful event brought the company's career to a sudden halt. It was 1648 and the ban on theatre had appeared to be easing. The King's Men ventured to present some plays at the Cockpit. Discretion was vital and by limiting the performances to a private audience they managed to remain there for four days. On the final day, they were in the middle of a performance of Fletcher's *Rollo, Duke of Normandy*, when disaster struck:

A party of foot soldiers beset the house, surprised 'em about the middle of the play, and carried 'em away in their habits, not admitting 'em to shift, to Hatton House then a prison, where having detained 'em sometime, they plundered them of their cloths and let 'em loose again.

The writer was James Wright, whose *Historia Histrionica* of 1669 was one of the first works of theatre history. Among the players arrested that day was John Lowin, who had joined the King's Men in 1603 and was now an elderly man. To be hauled off the stage and locked up, still in his costume, must have been a bitter end to his career. Indeed it was the sad end of a company of players who had been together in some form since the mid-1590s, when they were known as the Chamberlain's Men.

It was in the ranks of this remarkable company that William Shakespeare nurtured his writing, first adding the odd scene to works such as *Sir Thomas More* before soaring to the heights of his poetic power. Had he lived to see that fateful performance at the Cockpit he might have shaken his head in sadness at what had become of his old pals.

93. The First Female Actor to Perform In a Shakespeare Play Was Margaret Hughes in 1660

In 1629, just thirteen years after Shakespeare's death, the unthinkable happened on the English stage. Female members of Queen Henrietta Maria's troupe of French players joined their male colleagues on stage at the Blackfriars playhouse, scandalising the audience. On the continent it was quite normal for female parts to be played by women but it was a step too far in England. The crowd hurled apples at the performers, booing and hissing them off stage.

This bold attempt at dragging English theatre into the seventeenth century had failed. Female parts would never again be performed by women this side of the Civil War. But change was coming.

In the Johnson Museum of Art at Cornell University hangs a portrait of a woman wearing a low cut dress of rich amber silk and a little smile. Her dark ringlets frame a snow white face. This is Margaret Hughes, an actress who made theatre history when she became the first professional actress to appear in a Shakespeare play. The year was 1660 and Charles II had ascended the throne. He hated the idea of men playing female parts for two reasons: the onstage action was sometimes held up whilst the men shaved their beards off, but Charles also disliked the gender fluid connotations of men in dresses. From now on, he decided, only women could play women. That December, *Othello* was playing at the theatre in Vere Street, Covent Garden, and Margaret Hughes stepped onto the stage as Desdemona. Perhaps with the disaster of the French actresses at Blackfriars in mind, Margaret's debut was preceded with some specially written lines explaining to the audience how things stood now:

> I come, unknown to any of the rest,
> To tell the news; I saw the lady dressed.
> The woman plays today, mistake me not,
> No man in gown or page in petticoat.

The writer goes on to explain why this is a sensible development:

> To speak truth, men act, that are between
> Forty and fifty, wenches of fifteen;
> With bone so large, and nerve so incompliant,
> When you call 'Desdemona', enter a giant.

He had a point. Theatre had now entered a new era; indeed it never looked back. Margaret Hughes was a great success on the London stage and took a number of roles including that of Valeria in Aphra Behn's *The Rover*. She returned to the role of Desdemona in later years to the delight of Samuel Pepys who described her as a 'mighty pretty woman' and enthused about her 'dark ringletted hair and particularly good legs'.

For women of the seventeenth century a career on the stage was often a prelude to finding a rich husband or keeper and Margaret was no exception, becoming the mistress of Prince Rupert, the Duke of Cumberland. They were a glamorous pair, known for their extravagance and love of gambling. She died penniless in 1719 but has not been forgotten. Her pioneering role in English theatre was portrayed by Claire Danes in the film *Stage Beauty*.

94. THE ROLE OF OTHELLO WAS FIRST PLAYED BY A BLACK ACTOR IN 1833

These days it would seem unthinkable for the role of Othello to be played by a white actor. With black actors still under-represented on the London stage, this role is rightly reserved. It was not always thus. The days of white actors 'blacking up' in order to pass themselves off as Othello are not so far off – who could forget Laurence Olivier playing the title role in the 1965 film version, speaking in an 'exotic' accent with his face streaked in black make up. We may cringe today, but back in the swinging sixties things were even more difficult for black actors than they are today.

With this in mind it may surprise you that, as far back as 1833, there was a black actor in the role, and he caused a sensation.

Ira Aldridge was a black American actor who moved to the UK to pursue his career, seeing better opportunities in Britain than he did back home. While slavery was still legal in America, it had been abolished in Britain and the government was also about to extend the ban to the colonies. As he set sail for Liverpool it was his good fortune to become the personal attendant of the English actor James Wallack. Perhaps it was this connection which helped launch his British career. When Aldridge arrived he joined touring companies and travelled around England playing various roles. His lucky break came in March 1833 when the celebrated Shakespearean actor Edmund Kean collapsed on stage at the Theatre Royal in Covent Garden whilst playing Othello. Aldridge was asked to step in and became the first black actor in the UK to perform in that role. It was a scandal. Black faces were a common sight in the London of William IV but the bourgeoisie was not quite prepared to see one in a Shakespearean role. He faced a hostile press with reviewers incredulous that a black actor should be allowed to lay hands on the white actress playing opposite him. He was dismissed as 'Mr Wallack's black servant'. Audiences warmed to him however and his performance was eventually praised by *The Times*, who wrote, 'In *Othello*, Aldridge delivers the most difficult passages with a degree of correctness that surprises the beholder.'

Despite his pioneering role as the first black Othello, history had almost forgotten Ira Aldridge, until 2012 when he was the subject of a play at the Tricycle Theatre in North London. *Red Velvet* was written by the playwright Lolita Chakrabarti and told the story of Aldridge's extraordinary stage career and how he was received by white audiences. Chakrabarti's husband Adrian Lester played the lead role.

As for Ira himself? After his success in *Othello*, he went on to tour at the royal courts of continental Europe before returning to England and taking another iconic Shakespearean role – King Lear. He died in Poland in 1867 and is buried in the city of Lodz.

95. Shakespeare Has Been Translated into Eighty Languages, Including Klingon and Esperanto

When Shakespeare was writing his tragedies, histories and comedies he had a domestic audience in mind. Whether performing at the playhouse for the groundlings or at court for kings, queens and nobility, he was focussed on an English crowd and, especially, the English language.

His world was a small one. He could not have known that 400 years after his death, his name would be famous around the four corners of the globe, and that his characters would speak in strange accents and tongues he had never heard of.

So far, Shakespeare's work has been translated into a whopping eighty languages, including Cornish and Faroese. Other languages include Tagalog and Gujarati, ensuring that plays such as *Hamlet* and *Romeo and Juliet* have reached Africa, Asia, the Americas and beyond. In 2012, Shakespeare's Globe embarked on a major project to produce each Shakespeare play in a different language. Theatre companies from around the world descended on the Bankside playhouse and performed the plays according to their own traditions and tastes. *All's Well that Ends Well* was given the Bollywood treatment with a Gujarati interpretation. *The Winter's Tale* was performed in Yoruba, and *Julius Caesar* went back to its Roman roots with a performance by an Italian company.

Not content with life on Planet Earth, he has also been translated for a slightly more alien audience, travelling to outer space where the Starship Enterprise patrols the galaxy. In 2000, Star Trek fans produced a translation of *Hamlet* in Klingon. It was a tongue-in-cheek attempt to restore Shakespeare to its 'original' language. According to the rules of Klingon grammar, Hamlet's famous speech begins not with 'to be or not to be,' but with the rather less catchy 'taH pagh taHbe'. It hasn't caught on.

If Klingon is too 'out there' you could always try Shakespeare in Esperanto, an entirely manufactured lingo based on the structure of the major European languages. In 2001 an Esperanto production of the play *King Lear* was performed in Hanoi, Vietnam. Esperanto performances are rare, however, so for those who are curious to see what Shakespeare looks like in this obscure language, you can always buy a copy of *Rego Lear, Rikardo Tria* or *La Komedio de Eraroj* (*King Lear, Richard III* and *The Comedy of Errors* to you and me).

Of course, it was Shakespeare himself who began the process of introducing other languages into his work. Act III, Scene IV of the play *Henry V* is spoken entirely in French. It is a comic scene in which the French princess Katherine is taught some English words by her maid Alice. With this in mind it is likely that he would heartily approve of seeing his plays performed in such a rich variety of languages.

Shakespeare may have begun life in a small corner of a small country off the north-west coast of Europe but he is now a truly international figure, whose genius is cherished by people all around the globe.

96. His Birthplace Was Saved for the Nation by Charles Dickens

Shakespeare's birthplace on Henley Street in Stratford upon Avon is such an iconic highlight of the Shakespeare tourist trail it is strange to think that it was once in danger of being dismantled and shipped off to the other side of the Atlantic Ocean.

When Shakespeare's father John died in 1601, William inherited the family home. As the eldest son, he was now head of the family. By this time, of course, he had purchased New Place, the fancy manor house down the road, and had no pressing need to move back into his childhood bedchamber. The little house at Henley Street was nothing compared to the space and luxury he was now accustomed to. Always a shrewd businessman, he rented part of it out to a certain Lewis Hiccox who turned it into a tavern called the Maidenhead. Shakespeare did not forget the welfare of his sister Joan, however, and allowed her to stay on a little adjoining cottage for the peppercorn rent of one shilling a year for the rest of her life. After Shakespeare's death the property passed to his daughter, Susannah, who bequeathed it to her daughter Elizabeth. She, in turn, passed it down to the descendants of Shakespeare's sister Joan.

By the 1840s years of neglect had reduced Shakespeare's childhood home to little more than a dilapidated hovel. Its illustrious past had seemingly been forgotten and it was in danger of falling into irreversible decay. Enter the American entertainer P. T. Barnum. Better known as one half of the Barnum and Bailey circus masters, Mr Barnum was a natural showman. His love of spectacle and sleight of hand was legendary; it was Barnum who introduced to the credulous public a mythical creature known as a 'Feejee mermaid', with its monkey's head and a mermaid's tail. Naturally, for someone so in thrall to show business Barnum was also something of a Shakespeare fan.

He loved the Bard so much, in fact, that he visited Stratford in 1844, where he realised that the house on Henley Street was up for sale. The British did not seem interested in the fate of this important piece of national heritage and Barnum considered purchasing it himself. He would dismantle it and rebuild it in New York. Needless to say, British pride was piqued at the suggestion that an American should make off with one of our treasures. A committee swung into action and organised fundraising events to save it for the nation. One of those who dipped into his pocket was the novelist Charles Dickens. On 16 September 1847 the group purchased the property for £3,000 and the Shakespeare Birthplace Trust was set up to administer and run it. Dickens continued to support the Trust, producing amateur performances of Shakespeare plays to raise funds towards its running costs.

Barnum was seen as a threat to our Shakespearean heritage in 1844, but it could also be said that he saved it too. After all, if that flamboyant American showman had not shown an interest in Shakespeare's house, we may not have done so either.

97. If It Wasn't for Shakespeare There Would Be No Starlings in New York

Our American cousins may have lost out on Shakespeare's birthplace but they gained something else instead – and it was not entirely welcome. One of the worst aspects of Shakespeare's legacy is the fact that parts of New England are now overcome with starlings.

Eugene Scheiffelin was a German immigrant to America whose enthusiasm for the Bard led him to take the extraordinary step in 1890 of importing 100 starlings from England and releasing them into Central Park, New York City. As a member of the New York Zoological Society and a keen Shakespeare fan his intention was twofold. On one hand he wanted to experiment with introducing non-native species into North America with the hope they would acclimatise, and on the other hand he wanted America to be home to all the birds which feature in Shakespeare.

Shakespeare's starling appears in only one play, *Henry IV: Part I*. Hotspur is having one of his rants about how he plans to plague the king by repeatedly mentioning his enemy's name:

> But I will find him when he lies asleep, and in his ear I'll holla 'Mortimer!' Nay, I'll have a starling shall be taught to speak nothing but 'Mortimer', and give it him to keep his anger still in motion.

American readers might smile wryly at this as starlings are plaguing the US too. Despite the starling's modest contribution to Shakespeare, it is having a fairly negative impact on the North American ecosystem.

When Scheiffelin released his flock of 100 starlings they bred rapidly, leading to a population explosion; America is home to approximately 200 million of the flying pests today, each competing with the local fauna for food. According to farmers they steal grain from cattle leading to a reduction in milk output. They cause damage to buildings by roosting in great flocks and corroding the fabric with their droppings. More seriously, they were responsible for a plane crash in Boston when a flock of starling were sucked into the engine in 1960.

It is fair to say the starling is not greatly loved in America. Indeed it is the only bird which is *not* afforded any state protection. Despite the attempts to reduce their numbers by poisoning and shooting, the starling is thriving stateside. The same cannot be said in Britain where, ironically, the starling is on the endangered list.

Other birds mentioned in Shakespeare are the kite, lapwing, pigeon, raven, cuckoo, eagle, mallard, sparrow, swan, chough, finch, partridge, kestrel, blackbird, dove, loon, magpie, phoenix, quail, vulture, cormorant, jay, falcon, goose, heron, pelican and owl. None of these have caused as much damage as the starling.

If it is any consolation to Americans dismayed by the invasion of their country by a non-native species, the 'favour' has gone both ways. Having been introduced from North America in the nineteenth century, the grey squirrel are said to have contributed towards the decline of the native red squirrel.

All's fair in love and war!

98. Shakespeare Gave Us a Tree on Primrose Hill

On 23 April 1864 a procession of working-class Londoners marched through the city streets accompanied by the music of pipes and drums. They held banners aloft and held up the traffic, almost bringing the capital to a standstill. It sounds like one of the protest marches which are an increasingly common sight in London but this was no such thing. This was a grassroots celebration of the great Bard on the 200th anniversary of his birth. In the absence of any official celebrations the Workingmen's Shakespeare Committee decided to take things into their own hands and organise something themselves. It was decided that they would plant an oak tree on Primrose Hill in Shakespeare's honour and sprinkle it with water from the River Avon.

The Times newspaper was not impressed. They wrote: 'On Sunday, a very feeble, and under almost all its aspects, a most ridiculous attempt was made to celebrate the birthday of our great poet, by what was called in the handbills a 'Working Men's Shakespeare Jubilee and Great National Festival.' You can almost see the sneer on the journalist's face. Mockingly, he described the participants as 'the usual idle stock of banner bearers, or harmless idiots'.

This ragtag band of brothers had gathered in Russell Square from one o'clock, heartily welcoming any who joined them. By two o'clock their numbers had swelled and they were ready to set off. *The Times* describes it as a thin procession of not more than 500 people, although other sources put it at 100,000. When they reached Primrose Hill, they planted the sapling, to an accompaniment of cheers and music. At this point a certain Mrs Bankes stepped forward and read out a letter from the Chartist poet Eliza Cooke. *The Times* reported that Mrs Bankes voice shook with nerves but magnanimously excused her on the basis that she may not have been used to speaking in public. It was now time to christen the tree with a sprinkling of Avon water, but there was a small hiccup. The bottle was corked and the organisers had difficulty finding anyone who would confess to carrying a corkscrew about his person. Eventually a corkscrew was found and the tree was duly sanctified.

To finish the ceremony, Eliza Cooke's especially composed poem was read aloud:

> With labour's sweat drop – England's richest gem
> Here do the people laud fame's greatest son.
> Bearing her scroll – to match our worshipped one
> Here do the people write with blazing pen:
> Shakespeare was born of England's working men.

Shakespeare was widely taught in Victorian schools but even then he was becoming an 'elite' pastime. By the 1960s the tree had died. It was replaced with another oak sapling in 1964, complete with plaque commemorating the extraordinary event which had taken place a century ago. The plaque is now missing but the tree lives on – a fitting tribute not just to Shakespeare but to those heroic working-class Londoners who claimed him as their own.

99. He Was Not for an Age but for All Time

Ben Jonson may have been locked in rivalry with Shakespeare but he was full of warm compliments for him after his death. In his eulogy to Shakespeare in the First Folio he describes him as being the 'soul of the age'. This is all very nice but he then goes on to say 'he was not of an age but for all time'. The two plaudits seem to contradict each other. To be the 'soul of the age' implies that his relevance was particular to his own era and, therefore, not easily translated across the centuries. Shakespeare probably thought of himself as a writer of his time. He was an entertainer who worked with what he had, be it a wooden playhouse or a royal dining hall. His audience was rooted in the here and now; they wanted drama that spoke to the concerns of everyday people in Elizabethan or Jacobean England. Many of the references within the plays are thought to be topical allusions, obscure to us in the twenty-first century but crystal clear to the original audiences. It is the same with the jokes. Some of them are incomprehensible to us without the aid of a guidebook, and yet the groundlings at the Globe would have roared with laughter.

There is, however, the merest hint that Shakespeare gave a thought to his future audiences. The first lines of Sonnet 107 appear to suggest his sharp awareness that time does not stand still; the earth is in a constant state of renewal.

Not mine own fears, nor the prophetic soul
Of the wide world dreaming on things to come ...

The very fact that Shakespeare has retained his popularity over the last 400 years is testament to the timelessness of his work. His plays are constantly being adapted and updated. Theatre companies have staged Shakespeare in countless different settings and eras, highlighting the ease with which it can be done. In 2011 when Kevin Spacey presented *Richard III* at the Old Vic in London he chose to set the action in the present day. He wore a military style outfit evoking the image of a Middle Eastern dictator. In 2013 the Royal Shakespeare Company staged *Julius Caesar* with an all-black cast. Set in modern day Africa, the production did a brilliant job of breathing new life into Shakespeare's tale of betrayal and usurpation. Shakespeare's Globe recently did *As You Like It* in Edwardian dress with the male cast members in checked waistcoats and bowler hats. The female members of the company wore long black dresses and carried umbrellas which they twirled to good effect.

All this proves that while the language of Shakespeare might be dated, his essence never changes. It seems his old rival Ben Jonson hit the nail on the head. Shakespeare truly is for all time.

100. If He Was Still Around Today He Would Be Writing Radio Plays

So William Shakespeare, the 'Sweet Swan of Avon', died 400 years ago. A lot has changed in that time and the modern theatre scene would be almost unrecognisable to the man who forged his career in rough and ready wooden playhouses, open to the elements and any scavenger who could afford to pay a penny.

It is fun to imagine what Shakespeare would be doing if he were alive today. His output was prolific and he knocked out his dramas with the masses in mind. He was a truly populist writer, an unashamed hack who could turn his hand to any subject and any audience. For this reason it is often suggested that a twenty-first-century Shakespeare would feel at home writing for a soap opera such as *Eastenders* or *Coronation Street*. Some of his fruitier characters would certainly be at home in either show.

He would make a great soap writer but he would also be perfectly suited to radio plays. Shakespeare was a man who painted pictures in words. He needed to be. After all, Elizabethans did not go to 'see' a play; they went to 'hear' one. Verbal imagery was important and Shakespeare certainly had a knack for it.

Consider these lines from *Macbeth*. Macduff has just heard that his wife and children have been brutally murdered in his absence from the castle. His grief is unspeakable and it is left to Malcolm to put his reaction into words:

> What, man! Ne'er pull your hat upon your brows;
> Give sorrow words: the grief that does not speak
> Whispers the o'er fraught heart and bids it break.
> > Malcolm, *Macbeth*, Act IV, Scene III

It is hardly necessary to see the action on stage to imagine how Macduff feels to hear such tragic news. You can almost see him hiding his eyes, trying not to weep in front of his macho friends.

Another straightforward example is in the play *Richard III*. It is the eve of the Battle of Bosworth; little does the king know that he is headed for disaster. Even his men can sense it: 'My Lord of Surrey, why do you look so sad?' Richard asks as they pitch their tents for the night. It is a common device used by writers of radio plays who signpost the narrative with these verbal clues. For Shakespeare it would have been an entirely natural thing to do. He could have had Macduff and Lord Surrey express their feelings in words but he understood that people do not always verbalise things. Sometimes our friends have to do it for us.

The genius of Shakespeare lives on so many years after his death because he knew us. He understood our human frailties, our desires and ambitions, our secret fears. So on that note let's raise a toast to the greatest writer who ever lived and all that he has given us. It is at the theatre where he truly comes alive, however, so, to paraphrase Hamlet, get thee to a playhouse!